Taipei, to-siā 台北多謝

陪你旅行當道地的台霸郎

HOW TO TRAVEL LIKE A LOCAL

男子的日常生活——

著

滷肉飯 LU ROU FAN

白飯淋上脂香肉汁，是任何山珍海味也比不上的台灣美味。

The unbeatable classic Taiwanese dish of tender-braised pork belly in a rich gravy, served over rice.

說起台灣之光，我推珍珠奶茶，無人不拜倒在這 Q 彈奶香下。
Bubble tea is the indisputable star of the Taiwanese food scene. Surely no one is able to
resist the fragrance of milk tea and the bouncy tapioca balls.

小黃，是台灣計程車的暱稱，也是穿梭台北大小巷道的任意門。

Siao Huang, or "little yellow", as they are referred to in Taiwan - these vibrant taxis can take you anywhere in Taipei.

機車，是台北人拿來罵人的話，也是台北人都曾並肩作戰的代步隊友。
Ji Che, or motorbikes, are the indispensable vehicles that Taipei-ers can't live without.
Did you know? "*ji che*" is also colloquial phrase used for "*a pain in the neck*" in Taiwan.

廟宇，是城市裡的心靈寄所。
These religious sites are woven into the fabric of city life — places for locals to refresh
their spirits.

饒河街觀光夜市
Raohe St. Night Market

米其林必比登

夜市是白日辛勤工作的人，夜裡覓食的樂園。
Food paradises for city dwellers to indulge themselves in a night of culinary exploration.

MADE IN TAIWAN，是我們的驕傲。

No shortage of masks - Taiwan even donated some to countries that needed them during
the COVID-19 pandemic. Citizens are proud of their 'Made in Taiwan' branded masks.

發票上的號碼，每到奇數月 25 日就成了彩票，是每 2 個月一次國民的小確幸。

Every receipt comes with an 8-digit codes that is played in the national lottery on the 25th
of every odd-numbered month. The prizes range from NT$ 200 to NT$ 10,000,000.

婚姻平權 MARRIAGE EQUALITY

2019年5月17日，台灣成為亞洲第一個同志婚姻合法化的國家。
On 17th of May, 2019, Taiwan became the first country in Asia to legalise same-sex marriage.

101，每一次在這拍下煙火代表一年又過了。
Once the tallest skyscraper in the world, now Taipei 101 is the centerpiece of firework displays every New Year.

序

3 年前寫完首爾後，兩人心裡都明白想著，未來若有機會出版第二本書，一定要是台北，希望能將我們心目中的台北做成一本書。

正好去年初再次收到男子製本所 J.J. 的來信，問起了新書計畫，也才有了此次與時報出版合作的機會。當時疫情讓所有人都待在原地，我們也有了更多時間重新認識自己生長的這塊土地，想著今年也許就是那最好的一年，我們能將心念許久的心願實現。

於是，2020 年我們調整了工作步調，在這一年裡我們發文少了，平時動態也安靜許多，因為兩人正沈溺於台北這座可愛的城市裡，無法自拔！

很高興為了籌備新書，反而讓我們有更多機會以不同視角去回味也再理解台北。新書取名《台北多謝》，其實最喜歡的唸法是以台語「TO-SIĀ」發音，也好似台語不輪轉的人說著「台北都市」，除了想謝謝這段期間給予我們幫助的所有人外，同時也想謝謝台北這塊土地，謝謝台北擁有如此包容與多元的文化，謝謝台北是如此獨一無二，如此孕育我們成為現在的我們。

台北適合生活，也適合旅行，就算從沒來過，也不需因陌生而感到害怕，古錐的台味讓人很快就能適應；走沒幾步路，就有超級便利的商店；旅店旁總有幾間道地的家常小吃；喜歡咖啡的人，咖啡店選擇多到你恨不得定居台北；還有曾被荷蘭朋友形容成未來科技的捷運，台北不只交通便捷，就算旅行預算不高，也能玩得心滿意足。

兩人當初在擬書綱時，也延伸出了台北印象與台北特輯，希望能藉由不同形式的內容，分享更多視角的台北日常生活，也希望與台北初次見面的你，能透過《台北多謝》對台北有更多了解；更希望曾與台北相識的你，能每翻一頁都將留下新的回憶。

台北多謝！謝謝你是我的家，也是我最深愛的城市，這點，我們竟然是到了長大後才深刻明白。

Eddie, Juju

Preface

Following our previous publication on Seoul three years ago, the two of us knew that if there was a chance to publish a second book, it would definitely be about Taipei. I've always dreamed that the Taipei in our hearts would one day be immortalised within a book.

At the beginning of 2020, we received another invitation from our editor J.J., to discuss potential ideas about a new publication. However due to the pandemic, the whole world stopped, forcing everyone to drop any travel plans. As a result, we had more time to re-explore the familiar places where we grew up and so thought that maybe this might be the year that we can finally realise our long-cherished dream. The pandemic meant that we had to adjust our work pace and were forced to reduce our workload. We also accommodated ourselves to adopt a quieter and simpler lifestyle. We were completely indulged in the city of Taipei.

Our new book Thank you Taipei, has given us more opportunities to revisit and explore Taipei from a different perspective. In fact, my preferred pronunciation of the book title is "*to-siā*" Taipei when read in Taiwanese. It also sounds similar to "*too-tshi*", which means city. As well as wanting to show gratitude and thanking everyone involved for their help with this book, we also wanted to thank the city of Taipei for its inclusivity and diverse culture and for being so unique and nurturing us into who we are now.

Taipei is a perfect city whether for residency, or for travel. Even for those who haven't yet visited, there's no need to be afraid of the unfamiliar. The warm personality of the Taiwanese people will make you feel at home. You'll find convenience stores around every corner, authentic street stalls, serving home cooked food around your hotel and amazing coffee shops that are perfect for a quick rest during a busy day of urban exploration. The city is well connected via the MRT, which was once described by our Dutch friends as "futuristic technology". The convenience of transport and affordable prices will definitely help you forget your troubles and enjoy a relaxing trip.

While drafting the outline of the book, we also decided to include two new sections: Impressions of Taipei and Special Taipei. We hope that these will give different and interesting perspectives on life in Taipei and introduce to those who are new to the city, the version of Taipei that we are familiar with. For those who are revisiting or perhaps have a longer history with the city, we hope that our writing not only resonates with you, but perhaps you'll pick up some places new from our book!

To-siā Taipei, thank you for being my home and my most beloved city. We didn't realise this until we grew up.

Eddie, Juju

Contents

「我要一杯不加糖的少冰混蛋汁。」騎車男子緩緩從車上下來，站到大姐前把錢給付了，很快果汁機攪拌的聲響停止了，客製的混蛋汁就做好了，男子隨即大口吸上，再滿足的離去。

已開業近 40 年的混蛋老闆果汁店，不是因為老闆很混蛋，而是這裡的果汁都能混著生蛋一起打，所以取名混蛋老闆果汁店。不只能加蛋，新鮮現打的果汁也都能調整甜度與冰塊，小小果汁店懷舊門面在巷弄裡現在看來反倒特別新鮮，玻璃櫥窗整齊排滿了天然香甜色調，想再加什麼水果都能和老闆說，我想混蛋老闆果汁店儼然已是小區裡不可多得的健康飲品選擇，夏天喝是既消暑又營養。

我們喜歡坐在攤前的小桌慢慢喝，那炎熱緩緩的時光，能回憶過往。

混蛋老闆果汁店
Hun Dan Lao Ban Juice Bar

台北市士林區承德路四段 10 巷 35 號
0952-900-818
10:30-21:00 closed on Mon

"Could I get a mixed-egg juice, without sugar and less ice?"

The man got off from his motorbike and walked over to the shopkeeper. Soon after he paid for his order, the sound of the blender stopped. His customised "mixed-egg" smoothie was ready. After a big slurp, he left with a satisfied look on his face.

The doors of "*Hun Dan Lao Ban Juice Bar*" have been open for business for nearly 40 years. It didn't get its name because the owner is a bastard (mixed-egg in Mandarin sounds the same as 'bastard'), instead, it's aptly named for what it sells - smoothies with raw eggs. Not only can you crack an egg into to your freshly made smoothie, but the drink can be made to order to suit your preferred sweetness and amount of ice.

There's a contrast between the glass cabinet displaying colourful and vibrant rows of fruit, and the rustic backdrop of the tiny store. Your drink can be personalised to include whatever you want, so long as the shopkeeper can make it. In the summer, the smoothies are especially popular with locals who see them as a healthy and nutritious way of staving off the summer heat.

We always like to sit on the bench in front of the stall, taking our time to enjoy the drinks. Slow summer days make for lovely memories.

若在台北你正好有一個上午或下午的空檔，那麼就來台北市立美術館看展吧！買一張 30 元的門票走進展間，好像遊覽世界各地，甚至穿梭古今時空腳步。

花了 2 年 4 個月於民國 72 年正式落成開館的台北市立美術館，共設計了四層的展示空間，也是台灣第一座現當代美術館，特別喜歡那簡約建築白系外觀與玻璃帷幕引入日光，讓作品與空間也自然流動對話著。

來過北美館無數次了，雖對於藝術有時甚難領悟，但每次想讓思緒放鬆，或感到苦悶時，就會走進北美館，讓自己沉浸在那無限想像的場域裡，曾經在此認識了江賢二對生命與自然的執意，也在此凝視布列松在中國的跨時代感受。

台北市立美術館
Taipei Fine Arts Museum
www.tfam.museum

台北市中山區中山北路三段 181 號
02-2595-7656
09:30-17:30（Sat 09:30-20:30）closed on Mon

If you happen to have a free morning or afternoon, why not swing by the *Taipei Fine Arts Museum* for an exhibition? Tickets are available for as little as NT$ 30（$1USD）giving you the chance to both transport yourself to bygone eras and catch up on contemporary scenes. Expect installations and masterpieces created not only by local artists but a pool of international talents.

Inaugurated in 1983 after a 30 month-long construction, the *Taipei Fine Arts Museum* became the first contemporary art museum in Taiwan. It consists of a four-storey exhibition venue with a minimal white façade contrasted by eye-catching glass windows which allow the light to perfectly frame the artworks within.

Even though I've had the pleasure of visiting the museum many times, the displays and exhibitions remain fresh, introducing new concepts that I still take some time to wrap my head around. When life becomes too stressful, I like taking refuge in the infinite imaginative space of the museum. It was here, that I first encountered Paul Chiang's determination for life and nature and witnessed the trans-century metamorphosis of China through the lens of Henri Cartier-Bresson.

距離日常生活圈稍遠的內湖，每次走進此區最頻繁目的地是文心藝所看展，重新規劃後辦過幾檔展覽都令人耳目一新，邀請來自世界各地當代藝術家，以藝術作品帶領觀者一同腦力激盪，目前維持每 3 個月更新一次。

位於夾層 2 樓的書店，有經營者歷時一年從世界各地搜集而來一本本限量，甚至已絕版的建築藝術外文書籍，書店以建築思潮、建築師作品集、建築師藝術家與攝影師間的關係分類陳列，也舉辦主題書展、講座等，是替城市注入一股全新能量，來這也能打開自己更多閱讀的可能。

作為展覽與書店催化體驗的 1 樓咖啡廳也絕對值得坐下一試，在這能吃到台北知名麵包店「Purebread」的牛奶吐司；甜食來自甜點名店「某某」；招牌卡布奇諾咖啡有著綿密細緻的奶泡，風味也相當出色。想想，在台北想看展，文心藝所總是一處令人心生期待的角落。

文心藝所
Winsing Art Place
Instagram winsingartplace

台北市內湖區民權東路六段 180 巷 10 弄 6 號
02-2790-2786
10:30-18:30

Every time we travel to *Neihu*, a district of North Taipei a short distance from the city centre, *Winsing Art Place* is our frequent destination. The exhibitions at *Winsing Art Place* always amazed us as they featured contemporary artists from all over the world which refreshed every three months. On the second floor sits a bookshop with a catalogue of limited-edition books sourced by the owner from around the globe, from architecture, the arts to photography - some of the books are even out of print. For some of the collections, *Winsing Art Place* sometimes holds themed book exhibitions or forums, offering city-dwellers a chance to catch up on some reading and renew their perspectives on arts and culture.

If you're feeling a bit peckish, why not check out the café on the first floor, where you can find some of the famous Japanese milk bread from *Purebread bakery* and pâtissière from *Quelques Pâtisseries*. Be sure to try one of their signature cappuccinos too! Besides the *Taipei Fine Arts museum*, the Winsing Art Place is another emerging art venue in Taipei that deserves recognition.

「國際標準定義，2 歲以上未滿 12 歲即為兒童。」縱使已成人許久，但想想每年都還是會去兒童樂園，陪著家人姪子、陪著已生兒育女的友人前往，雖台北現在的兒童新樂園早已不是兒時記憶裡的那個地方了，但每次陪伴著，總會想起那快遺忘的懵懂時光。

圓山舊址兒童樂園在被納入國定遺址範圍後，因諸多限制無法順利更新營運，因此市府重新規劃鄰近美崙公園的兒童新樂園，寬闊場域於 2014 年完工設計了 13 項遊樂設施，像是雲霄飛車、自由落體、海盜船等項目，皆是符合兒童可乘載的程度。

兒童新樂園

Taipei Children's Amusement Park

www.tcap.taipei

台北市士林區承德路五段 55 號
02-2833-3823 #105、106
09:00-17:00

想想以前可沒有這麼多設施，也沒有像戰火金剛這種巨型搖控的機器人；以前更沒有偌大的建築物裝滿各式的商店，總覺得像兒童新樂園這樣的場所，其實是大人私心打造來滿足所有大朋友的回憶，能在陪伴的同時，重溫過去時光，也留下屬於此刻的美好。

每次走進園區，沉浸在五顏六色運行旋轉，聽見此起彼落的歡笑尖叫，大腦像是不知覺跟著分泌快樂的多巴胺、心情也跟著微笑，這裡是被天使守護的領域，長大後還能在兒童新樂園待上一天，是很幸福的事。

"*According to the international standard, individuals between the age of 2 and 12 are considered children.*" Be that as it may, we still visit the *Taipei Childen's Amusement Park* every year with my nephews and nieces, or friends who have children. After the amusement park was refurbished, it no longer resembles the one from my childhood memory, but its still a good place for reminiscing about good memories from the past.

After the park on the old site was designated as a national ruin, it struggled to keep up with renovations until eventually *Taipei City Hall* planned for its relocation to a new spot adjacent to *Meilun Park*. The new park was completed in 2014, complete with 13 additional facilities such as a new roller coaster, free fall machine, pirate ship and other popular rides.

Thinking about it, the old park actually felt like a private park that was a secret among lucky children. It didn't have many facilities - no giant remote-controlled robots like *King Kong*, no buildings filled to the brim with shops, but that didn't stop it from becoming every child's paradise. Whether you visit the park with friends old or new, it's clear that just being here will revive old memories while giving life to new ones.

Every time I enter the park, the brilliant lights from the forest of colourful machines, accompanied by screaming and laughter, synchronised with the motion of the rides, always gets my blood pumping.

It's heartwarming to think that with its life renewed, the amusement park can continue to give happiness and laughter to the young, while helping old children like us relive our innocent childhoods.

近幾年台北掀起小吃升級的風潮，在懷舊新穎空間裡，賣著創新台味小吃，像是以傳統滷味為招牌的渣男、結合串燒炸物的饞食坊，還有以肉燥麵私房菜著稱的酒菜市場都相當受歡迎，沒預先訂位時常不得其位。

三間裡以酒菜市場資歷最新，卻最符合我心中小吃攤的本色，坐在拼接木板而成的工作檯吃飯，也彷彿回到巷弄裡的小吃攤。來這想配酒就點 鹹豬肉，又鹹又甜的，肉有嚼勁又軟嫩，再配上一旁的生菜，好新好台的滋味；不然點份蜜汁魚與炸起司片也行，酥脆起司濃香，魚乾嚼阿嚼太爽快；如果會餓，就先來一碗 Q 彈有勁的肉燥麵，肉燥醬汁滾滿麵條，好

酒菜市場
Jiucai Market
Instagram jioutsai_market

台北市中山區中山北路二段 77 巷 25-1 號
02-2581-7579
17:30-01:00

香又飽足；愛吃辣就淋點自製辣椒，辛香不麻的那種。

喝什麼酒好，台啤是基本款，偶爾還有不在酒單上的特調，這裡每道料理都好細膩，是老闆曾在西式餐廳廚房工作累積扎實功力功不可沒，而店內不同曲風歌單，特別輕鬆、也特別愜意。

想想台北人的確愛極了小吃攤，只是一般來說路邊小吃店第一較不整潔，第二整體環境樸素屬於快速果腹就離開，實在不宜久坐，也難以為慶祝聚會場所，所以當升級版的小吃料理店出現，有下酒菜又有酒，也能好好吃頓飯，著實替台北食客們帶來不同的曙光。

In the recent years, Taipei has been hit with a new food trend, consisting of elevated street foods - restaurants with vintage interiors serving well-loved Taiwanese cuisine with a modern twist, such as *Taiwan Bistro's lu wei* (an assorted platter of soy-braised meats and vegetables), *Chan Shih Fang's yakitori* and *tempura*, and *Jiucai Market's* signature braised pork mince noodles. Make sure you book a table in advance before visiting one of these popular spots.

Jiucai Market is the youngest amongst the three places mentioned above, and in my opinion, is the most authentic. Sitting on one of their workbenches, spliced together with wooden planks, is reminiscent of the the food stalls that one could find in the many alleyways of old Taipei. The salted pork serves as a perfect savoury accompaniment to booze. The meat is chewy but tender, and the lettuce served on the side is perfect to freshen up the palate. Also worth mentioning, is their honey-glazed fish jerky and slices of fried cheese. For the famished, the kitchen will also happily rustle up a hearty bowl of braised pork mince noodles. These noodles are coated with a thick and deliciously rich gravy that is the very definition of comfort food. Fancy a little kick? Just drizzle in some of the fiery homemade chilli oil (they're the kind that is spicy, but not numbing).

As for drinks? On offer of course, is the essential Taiwan Beer and sometimes, even cocktails are served. The owner of Jiucai Market's honed his skills at western fine dining restaurants before setting up this establishment and his skills are evident in every single dish that the restaurant serves.

People in Taipei really do love street food stalls, but unfortunately many see them as unhygienic, and seating can be quite limited (if there is even any at all). These reasons mean that street stalls aren't really a place for friends or family to gather. Therefore, with the advent of new restaurants like *Jiucai Market* who sell the familiar flavours of Taiwan's street food stalls, but offered in a comfortable environment, you can imagine the disruption to Taipei's food scene.

「聞著水果氣味，再想像最契合的茶香，這樣想著很快就有了每一塊蛋糕的雛形了。」 Cypress & Chestnut 主理人 YiLing 因為喜歡水果，所以在這總有不同水果製成的時令鮮果蛋糕。

冬天除了草莓外，也曾將哈密瓜與橘子入甜；夏天盛產的芒果外，也曾嘗試以水蜜桃與荔枝做成夾餡或裝飾，一年四季都美味的檸檬與葡萄，就成了店裡的經典味道。

Cypress & Chestnut

Instagram cypress_chestnut

台北市大安區復興南路二段 148 巷 5 號 1 樓
reservation only

覺得做蛋糕是日子裡最放鬆的時刻，或許也正因為如此，Cypress & Chestnut 1 週通常只開放 2 至 3 天內用，其餘時間 YiLing 都讓自己沉浸在香甜裡，準備客人預訂的蛋糕。

開業至今，Cypress & Chestnut 總給人一種慢裡優雅的韻味，但想在這裡內用實在很難預約，所以我們更常是趁預訂友人的生日驚喜，讓每每嚐著那誘人的水果鮮奶油蛋糕，總好像也感受到最簡單想念的香甜氣息。

"*When I smell fruit, I always try to imagine what tea might suit it, and that's usually enough to bring to mind the recipe of a cake*", says Yi Ling, the owner of *Cypress & Chestnut*, who is absolutely bananas for fruit. Yi Ling styles her creations according to the seasons - in winter, strawberries, honeydew melons and tangerines are used, while mangoes, peaches and lychees become the foundation in the summer months. Fruits that are available all year round, such as lemons and grapes, are familiar flavours for most of the cakes here.

Cypress & Chestnut only opens to dine-in customers 2 to 3 days per week. If you're lucky to visit during the rest of the week, you'll find the store alive with sweet buttery fragrances, as Yi Ling spends this time baking pre-ordered cakes for eager customers. Baking is when Yi Ling feels the most relaxed, and so she decided to run the restaurant on this schedule, resulting in her cakes being highly exclusive!

Since it opened its doors over two years ago, *Cypress & Chestnut* has rightfully established a reputation for delivering quality cakes that will leave you *s-peach-less!* It can be quite hard to book a table, so usually we only come for birthdays. If you're in the area, be sure to pop by for some of Yi Ling's divine fruit shortcakes!

在台北的朋丁總是有書、有展覽，也有能坐下來嚐份咖啡沉澱日子的獨立
空間。　3 層樓的老房座落於台北極富文藝氣息的中山靜巷，1 樓為書店，
集結國內外超過 200 種視覺藝術類型的書籍雜誌，像是台灣旅店出刊的地
方誌《about:》、德國出版圍繞茶事的《Journal du The》和朋丁發行的合
作繪本與攝影集等，書架上陳列著為數眾多的獨立出版刊物，都是在台北
其它書店極為少見的。

朋丁

Pon Ding

Instagram pondingspace

台北市中山區中山北路一段 53 巷 6 號
02-2537-7281
11:00-20:00 closed on the last Mon of the month

2 樓是與 Pharos Coffee 一起規劃的咖啡空間，供應手沖單品與義式咖啡
外，也有不是咖啡的飲品，也能將 1 樓的書籍帶至 2 樓閱讀，來這選上一
個角落待著，倚著一整面窗的明亮，感受那股清透的藝文氣息。

3 樓展覽空間總有令人驚喜的藝術作品，這裡就像是台北城市裡的一處綠
洲，有時當自己感到靈感匱乏時，便會獨自來到朋丁，總能拾獲無限的想
像與期待。

This serene store offers books, exhibitions and good coffee - therefore everything that describes a perfect spot for a tranquil day in Taipei.

Transformed from an old apartment building, *Pon Ding* is hidden away in a undisturbed alley in *Zhongshan* district, famous for its artistic and hipster vibes. The ground floor is a bookshop, boasting a collection of 200 books and magazines related to the visual arts and design, including 《about:》 from Taipei, the German publication 《Journal du The》 which focuses on tea culture. It also stocks books on illustration and photography published through joint efforts between *Pon Ding* and their partners. The shelves of this hidden gem are filled to the brim with the works of many independent publishers, making this a must visit location for rare book hunting.

On the second floor, you'll find the *Pharos Coffee* shop, offering a range of caffeinated and non-caffeinated beverages. After some interesting finds on the ground floor, why not bring them upstairs, order a coffee and find a quiet spot to sit back and immerse yourself in some reading?

Expect some surprises on the third floor - this is where you'll find *Pon Ding's* exhibition gallery which is like an oasis in the city of Taipei. Sometimes when I lack inspiration, I'll come to *Pon Ding* just for this space alone.

十間茶屋的出現，替台北茶界帶來顛覆傳統的美學想像。全白視覺是一改刻版印象裡的大膽色調；街角透光玻璃屋，大概也是城中最美的角落了。從小在製茶人家長大的店主 Franco，對茶葉的烘焙與萃取也很有一套，店內供應熱泡、熱沖冰、冷泡、冰滴 4 種風格的茶品。

不只將美引入茶的世界，也將茶味視覺化。在這自製的台灣冷泡茶是裝進透明玻璃瓶身，茶色由淺而深分為「00、05、10」，也代表著茶葉烘焙與

十間茶屋
Shi Jian Tea

www.shijiantea.com
Instagram shijiantea

台北市信義區忠孝東路四段 553 巷 48 號
02-2746-5008
11:30-20:00

發酵程度，時常來到台北松菸閒逛想喝杯清爽的茶飲，就會走進這座透明森林，點一瓶坐下歇息，或外帶邊走邊飲都好。

最愛「10」暮色小葉紅，以小葉種烏龍茶樹製成紅茶，昏黃色澤裡是層次飽滿，回甘甜味如情人道別的濕吻，讓人依依不捨，原來以茶去想像回味著，也能是件如此浪漫的事。

Shi Jian Tea offers a new perspective on traditional teahouses in Taipei. The glass-clad store is fronted by a snow-white façade - a bold palette for a tea brewing affair.

Owner Franco comes from a family of tea growers and specialists, and is not a stranger to the process of tea roasting and extraction. The cumulation of his expertise has led to the four different types of tea featured on the menu of *Shi Jian Tea - hot brew, brew over ice, cold brew* and *ice drip.*

Not only does *Shi Jian Tea* bring new aesthetics to the tea-drinking world, but their operation also visualises the tea-drinking experience. The cold brew tea, made using locally sourced Taiwanese tea, is housed in a clear glass bottle. The colour of the tea brew is categorised by its different degrees of roasting and fermentation, from light in complexion to heavy and dark - represented in house as *00, 05* and *10.* Whenever you swing by the *Song Shan Cultural Park* and feel like a refreshing cup of tea, this beautiful tea house will always be ready for you. Feel free to sit inside, enjoying each sip, or take away to accompany you on your stroll.

Our favourite from *Shi Jian* is the Black Oolong tea, a type of black tea sourced from *Nantou* in the centre of Taiwan, famous for its alluring rich golden honey-like complexion. The sweet and mellow aftertaste has been likened to a romantic kiss from your beloved.

HOT BREW   90
BREW OVER ICE   95
COLD BREW   95
ICE DRIP   150

想要來一趟茶旅行，無須走入山野茶園，待在城中的三徑就荒也能心領神會。以老木、水泥、紗布、陶器構成的茶館，讓空間注入質樸古韻，向街的落地窗將陽光和煦留在空氣裡，同時也讓茶的光景走進行人日常，在這找個舒服的角落坐下，茶席備好了，就開始泡茶吧！

來這，就算你對茶學一無所知，也能自己沖出一杯好喝的茶。茶館內有專業茶師示範，在這泡茶有一套系統，讓你能嚐到每支茶葉最理想的風味。更跳脫傳統茶藝精神，也沒所謂框架，品茶配傳統鬆糕合味，想搭饅頭或

三徑就荒

Hermit's Hut

www.hermits-hut.com
Instagram hermits_hut

台北市信義區忠孝東路四段 553 巷 46 弄 15 號 1 樓
02-2746-6929
11:00-20:00（Mon&Thu13:00-）closed on Tue

西式馬卡龍也都行，或新或舊的儀式，皆是感受茶千變萬化的滋味，時而溫柔清雅，也時而剛毅厚實。

品牌也推行月付茶誌販售，讓會員每月收到不同茶葉，包裹內附沖泡教學卡與製成說明，不只習茶該有的味道，也熟識各種茶葉。主理人 Vicky 從小便深覺台灣茶比西洋茶更美、也更有意思，不該只是年長者的愛好，因此習茶十幾年後便成立了三徑就荒，在這，茶好像與生活有了更輕鬆、更生活的連結。

There is no need to go into the mountains for a tea journey - *Hermit's Hut* in central Taipei can offer you the spiritual voyage that accompanies a heavenly brewed cup of tea. With its tones of old wooden furniture, concrete, linen curtains and pottery, brightened by the large floor-to-ceiling windows, the tea house is filled with a sense of modesty. If you're interested, come in, find yourself a comfortable corner and let's start brewing tea!

You don't need any prior knowledge of the tea ritual to come here - you'll still be able to brew a pot of delicious tea for yourself. A team of in-house tea specialists will demonstrate the process to you, making sure you taste the ideal flavour of every tea. Tea served in this manner is usually paired with traditional Taiwanese rice pastries, but visitors can also choose an accompaniment of either *mantou* (Chinese steamed buns) or macarons for the sweet-toothed.

Co-founder Vicky has preferred Taiwanese tea over Western tea since she was a kid, but was once a firm believer that tea drinking is for the elderly. After mastering her skills under a number of experts over the last 15 years, she eventually co-founded *Hermit's Hut*, with the aim of making the process of brewing and drinking high quality tea, a more casual and approachable leisure activity for people from all walks of life.

最常推薦給外國友人的台北餐館，大概就屬貓下去敦北俱樂部了。友人也
愛問，那來這要點什麼？我會說，菜單上有興趣的都可一試啊！

早年「貓下去」還在徐州路時，西式小館裡有義大利麵、有燉飯，還是離
不開眾人印象裡的西餐；2016 年遷店來到敦化北路後，整間店氣氛不同
以往了，就連菜色也變了不少，是將西餐館重新解構定義。

滿櫃的精釀啤酒先點上一瓶，再來一份冠軍薯條是熟客開吃的起手式。喜
歡三明治的，招牌 BLT 還在；愛吃牛肉的，可以點烤牛排；想試試麵飯，

貓下去敦北俱樂部

Meowvelous

Instagram meowvelousinc

台北市松山區敦化北路 218 號
02-2717-7596
11:00-15:00, 17:30-00:00

來份台西合壁的 XO 醬擔仔麵，或台式便當榨菜排骨飯；還有像涼麵這種
街頭又台式復古的小吃，重新詮釋後竟也做得如此美味；你會發現當時代
在變，貓下去敦北俱樂部也默默地齊行，創造屬於這世代的台北味覺，是
非常有意思的。

這裏有好玩的酒，讓人嘖嘖稱奇的食物，跟輕鬆時髦的氛圍，成功地將城
裡每顆疲累的心都給撫慰了。

Meowvelous has earned a position on our list of must-go places in Taipei for bringing friends new to Taiwan. What's our recommendation? Literally anything on the menu. What started on *Xuzhou road* as a casual spot for pasta and risotto has since relocated to *Dunhua North Road* in 2016, and has blossomed into an cultural establishment that strikes a balance between Western and Taiwanese cooking styles.

Expect to find a selection of beers from independent breweries and make sure to try the signature *Meowvelous Fries*. There are plenty of options on the menu, whether you're after a good sandwich or steak, but the signature dishes of *Meowvelous* are the innovative Taiwanese dishes such as *XO-sauce Danzai Noodles*, *Pork Chop Bento with pickled mustard greens* or *street-food style cold noodles*. Here, traditional classics have been given a modern twist while maintaining their familiarity and tastiness. Even as the trends move on, *Meowvelous* has continued to make an impression on the Taipei palate with their interpretations of fusion cuisine.

Interesting alcohol, stunning cuisine and overall a very fashionable atmosphere, makes Meowvelous an unmissable destination for exhausted urban individuals looking for something new.

在台北想吃漢堡，就會想起漢堡俱樂部。兩位七年級生老闆 ED 與何煒從漢堡餐車開始，當時一台很酷的福斯經典古董車，每日載著限量供應的手作漢堡，可說是征服了不少漢堡迷的胃，兩人最後不再隨機出沒，決定落腳大安區巷弄成立漢堡俱樂部。

不只食物香氣引人著迷，美式摩登復古氛圍，響起了各式曲風音樂，十足西方影集裡才會出現的快餐場景，熱鬧極了。

漢堡菜單上維持七、八種口味，甚至還有素堡，偶爾也加碼推出新餐。記憶裡的炸雞堡，是有豐富酸甜風味；招牌必點牛肉排，熟度細膩拿捏，是鮮腴多汁又好香；現炸薯條撒上香料調味，辛香甜鹹口味實在特別；除了可樂，還有奶昔、西瓜汁、咖啡、啤酒等做解膩搭配。不敢說這裏是台北城裡最好吃的漢堡店，不過絕對是名列前茅，令人念念不忘的那種。

漢堡俱樂部
Everywhere burger club

Instagram everywheretpc

台北市大安區光復南路 420 巷 21 號
02-2704-6825
11:30-15:00, 17:00-22:00（Fri&Sat-22:30）closed on Mon

Whenever we're in the mood for a great burger, the *Everywhere Burger Club* immediately comes to mind. What originally started out as a mobile burger van in a cool, retro Volkswagen, gained so much popularity with burger fanatics, that owners Ed and Wei Ho eventually decided to transform the business into what is now a beloved diner located in the *Da'an district*. Hearty food, combined with American vibes and a backdrop of classic tunes, has made this diner resemble something from Hollywood movies.

The kitchen serves 7 to 8 styles of burgers, including vegetarian options. If you're lucky, on occasion, the menu features new trial items. The recently introduced fried chicken burger gives mouthful after mouthful of balanced sweet and sour pleasure. Their signature beef patties are overflowing with juices and are perfect when accompanied with their generously seasoned and herby fries. As for the drinks? On offer are a choice of coke, milkshakes, watermelon juice, coffee or beer to stave off the grease and fat.

We don't dare to say that this is the best burger joint in town, but it's definitely up there on the list with the most unforgettable ones!

Delicate Antique 的店主因為喜歡古道具，所以開了一間古物店，聽起來順理成章；但能讓就算不是熱衷老件的人也走進去，那就另當別論了，我會說那是一種時光停留的魔力。

這裏收藏的古物，早期以日本風格古道具為主，近幾年店主旅行地圖也擴及歐美地區，所以也能看見來自西方的藝術品和家具，甚至也有越來越多的現代設計師桌椅入列。

有的是來歷可考的物件，有的像是無名雕像只留下斑痕的滄桑，這裡頭的古物堆滿的歲月或許能以千萬年計算，三角屋頂的矮白房，就像是台北城裡訴說老件人生的博物館，隨時有好奇的人探訪。

Delicate Antique

Instagram delicate_antique

台北市大安區嘉興街 346 號
02-8732-5321
12:00-20:00 closed on Mon

Delicate Antique is the result of the owner's lifelong passion for collecting vintage items. With its magic power brought out by time, the store not only attracts like-minded people but those who are lured in through curiosity.

Originally, the collection focused on old Japanese items, but recently, they've expanded to collecting art and crafts, homeware products and designer furniture from Europe and the Americas - fuelled by the owner's frequent journeys abroad.

Some items are age-certified, while others were created by anonymous masters of their crafts with their exact birthdate unknown - but one thing for sure is that the combined age of the collection can be counted in the many hundreds of years. All of these treasures are housed within a small white building, with a characteristic gable roof, like a time capsule with white walls, luring passersby into an alternate reality of the capital.

初見北門鳳李冰時，以為指的是台北北門，後來才得知是來自宜蘭北門，東部地方特色冰品來到台北東區裡轉眼也過了 8 個年頭，低調門面沒什麼裝潢，若不是有塊招牌寫著店名，路過還真會以為只是一般住家民宅呢！

這裡的冰令我想起兒時常買的叭噗，特別綿密滑順，除了鳳李冰與荔枝冰只出單杯外，其餘口味皆能一次兩種混搭。自己最愛芋頭冰，因需每天一早以新鮮芋頭加糖加水現打製作，所以通常都會晚半個小時出場，綠豆沙也是。渾然天成的自然清爽，一次將兩種口味送進嘴裡時，瞬間盈滿唇齒與鼻腔間，沒有太過濃郁香氣反倒顯得純粹，不只真材實料給得也扎實，符合市井小民的銅板價，也是每次東區飯局結束後，最無經濟負擔的續攤首選。

北門鳳李冰
Bei Men Feng Li Bing

台北市大安區忠孝東路四段 216 巷 33 弄 9 號
02-2711-8862
12:00-21:30

When I first saw the words *"Bei Men (North Gate) Feng Li Bing"*, I first thought that it was something referring to the iconic North Gate of Taipei, turns out it was in reference to North Gate of Yilan! This northeastern brand has actually been around in the capital for eight years, with an inconspicuous store front - if it wasn't for the sign above the store, you'd just think it was an ordinary residential building!

Bei Men Feng Li Bing's ice creams remind me of the *"ba boo"* that I frequently bought from as a kid. *Ba boo* is a traditional Taiwanese ice cream cart that was pulled by a bicycle and whose namesake is an onomatopoeia of the honking sound the bike would make as it circled residential blocks. The ice cream sold by these mobile vendors were beloved by people of all ages, and were particularly smooth and creamy. Except for single-cup 'feng li bing' (pineapple and perilla plum) and lychee flavours, all of the other flavours can be mixed and matched. My personal favourite is the taro flavour. The taro ice cream from here is made fresh every morning and contains only fresh taro, sugar and water. Because making it is a time consuming process, it's usually available half an hour after the other flavours, as is the case of the mung bean ice cream.

Feng Li Bing's refreshing ice creams are all made from natural ingredients. Every spoon of their ice creams are a delight that fills the mouth with a fruity and creamy goodness. The ice creams are perfect intense explosions of flavour, but aren't too rich.

2013 年台北捷運信義線象山站開通後，所有人與象山的距離自此更近了，出站步行小段卽能抵達健行步道口，山腳下一間阿婆的飲料礦泉水小攤，定時開張正好也成了過路山友們的水份補給站。

400 公尺處的六巨石我想是大多數台北人上山的目的地，雖地圖解說牌上標示約 15 分鐘步行時間，但我認為是按平時有運動習慣的人給的參數，不過就算極度缺乏運動，其實沿著步道緩緩而上應該也不出 30 分鐘，想想，只有海拔 181 公尺的象山眞是一座極度友善城市人的山啊！

象山
Elephant Mountain

總是習慣在接近傍晚出發，就能一次拾獲台北白晝與向晚的點滴況味。攀上巨石等著天色由蔚藍漸層至落日薄霧籠罩只餘光影，從未見過如此美的台北，也是在山底下無緣見著的風光。

巨石區有一條通往市立聯合醫院松德院區的小徑，稍微走下就少了枝葉遮避，此面一望無際台式高矮樓房不禁回憶，以前站得低總覺得台北景致比不上異國，然而日子久了才明白，我們只是時刻身處於其中而不知，台北實在美極了。

Since the completion of the Taipei Metro Xinyi red line in 2013, the popular hiking trail up *Elephant Mountain* has become even easier to get to. The start of the trail is only a short walk from the exit of the *Xiangshan metro station*. At the base of the mountain, is a stall that is ran by a friendly old lady, stocking a variety of items that are useful for the hike. Frequent hikers up *Elephant Mountain* will tell you about their friendship with her.

The 400m checkpoint called the *Six Giant Rocks*, is the goal for most hikers. Despite many maps suggesting that it takes 15 minutes to reach this point, beginners should probably be prepared for a longer hike. However, even at a slower pace, most people should be able to reach it within 30 minutes. With an elevation of only 181 metres, *Elephant Mountain* is a highly approachable hiking trail suitable for urbanites.

We prefer visiting the mountain in the early evening hours, for a lovely view of the Taipei basin under both day and night light. Sitting on the giant rocks on the mountain, you'll witness the beautiful transition of the blue sky gradually turning to an autumnal orange. At the *Six Giant Rocks*, there's also a small path that leads towards the *Taipei City Psychiatric Center*. This small trail is discrete and not many people know of it - but for those that know, it affords a much clearer view of the Taipei skyline. Like most people, we used to value trips abroad more than local trips, but it's only when you explore more of Taipei, that you realise how beautiful the city is.

不只是圖書館原為台北的設計圖書館，後來搬遷易名重新規劃品牌識別，
雖名稱跳脫了設計二字，但其本質不變，這裡擁有超過一萬本藏書與期
刊，同樣以設計藝術生活類別為主，多見中英日三種語言。採單日售票入
館可在場內自由取閱櫃上書籍，填寫資料入會後也能外借書籍一週。票卡
設計也頗具巧思，仔細一看集結不同領域職人的推薦書單，讓票券多了一
份知識傳遞的有趣意義。

不只是圖書館
Not Just Library
Instagram notjustlibrary

台北市信義區光復南路 133 號
02-2745-8199#322
10:00-18:00 closed on Mon

館內分為三個閱讀空間，有新建寬闊的書池與日治時期留下的女湯澡堂，
而戶外花園是能舒緩雙眼筋骨的短暫小旅。「讀書前，請先沐浴」因澡堂
風格相當受時下群眾歡迎，建議平日來能較愜意，可以好好讀幾本書，聽
聽音樂，泡在書本裡的世界，也洗淨心中的喧囂。

Not Just Library, is a library originally dedicated to design lovers in Taipei. Later, it was relocated and renamed as a more museum-oriented venue for brand identity. Although the name has escaped the word 'design', the establishment remains faithful to its original concept. *Not Just Library* stocks more than 10,000 publications and journals, with a focus on the arts, with text in Chinese, English and Japanese.

With a single day ticket, you can enter the venue and spend some time browsing their selection of books. If you find something interesting, you can also borrow them for up to two weeks - simply sign up for the free membership. Just like the venue's name, the artistically designed entry ticket is not just a ticket, but curiously includes a recommended reading list consisting of renowned Taiwanese authors.

Not Just Library is subdivided into three reading spaces - a newly opened spacious '*book pond*', the '*book bathhouse*' transformed from a womens '*sento*' (a Japanese communal bathhouse) and finally an outdoor garden designed to offer more natural light to revitalise tired eyes. "*Before you read, please take a shower*" is the slogan that perfectly encapsulates the bathhouse setting of the venue and immediately drew public attention when it first opened. To avoid the venue at its busiest, it's recommended to visit on weekdays, when you can pick up a few books, listen to some music, and more comfortably catch up on some reading.

旅行走過亞洲幾座城市後，想想還是屬家鄉台北三更半夜的美食最多，若不想去夜市人擠人，還有像永和豆漿大王這種 24 小時營業的點心店，樸質清爽的口味，最適合半夜有點嘴饞，而可多可少的份量，也相當友善獨身人士。

在台北大安開業 30 年的永和豆漿大王品項琳瑯滿目，來過幾次後覺得店內的燒餅油條夾蛋最合我意，蓬鬆酥餅在嘴中意外越嚼越濕潤有味；再來是小籠包，Q 彈厚皮包進扎實層次肉料，放進嘴裡咬破時總有鮮香的湯汁。

永和豆漿大王

Yonghe Soy Milk King

台北市大安區復興南路二段 102 號
02-2703-5051
24 hrs

許多人來這也會點鹹豆漿，但實在太容易飽，所以自己通常會選單純的熱豆漿，豐稠微甜有純淡的豆香，都是店內師傅每天慢活細工製作。

除了宵夜，接近晨昏是兩個最熱鬧的時刻，常常騎樓下擺滿鐵桌坐滿了食客，也不少人外帶。城裡有許多像永和豆漿大王這樣的豆漿店，明明不在永和，卻以此地命名，其實是豆漿店起源地名永和，現已更像是美味豆漿店的代稱了。

After travelling through several cities in Asia, we think our hometown of Taipei offers the most food options to fulfil midnight cravings. Don't want to pop down to the local night markets? There're also spots like *Yonghe Soy Milk King*, which opens 24-hours and serves a wide range of small and tasty dishes. If you're feeling peckish at night, this is the place to come to. The small portion sizes mean that it's also perfect for solo eaters.

The *Yonghe Soy Milk King* has been open for business for 30 years in the *Da'an district* of Taipei and has been offering a tasty menu for just as long. Our favourite is the *shao bing you tiao* which consists of a deep-fried dough stick and egg, rolled into a perfectly fluffy and flaky flatbread. Another famous dish is the *xiao long bao*, a Chinese soup dumpling that is made by wrapping a delicious parcel of pork meat and soup broth inside a skin-thin layer of soft pastry.

The salty soy milk is one of the most popular items here, while we find it a bit too filling. Why not try the hot plain soy milk instead? The soy milk here is prepared fresh in-house every day and it has a reputation for having a naturally sweet and fragrant soybean flavour.

Interestingly, the early morning and late evening periods are when the *Yonghe Soy Milk King* are the most lively. Visit during these hours are you'll often see the metal tables downstairs full of diners, with many queuing up for take away as well.

Taipei has many soy milk shops that are similar to *Yonghe*, but none of which can replace this establishment. In fact, the name "*soy milk king*" has now become more than just a store name, but a synonym for the high quality and delicious soy milk stores through the city.

內用
Eat H

在台北還有一種吃食必嚐,那就是牛肉麵,各門各派繽紛口味從清燉、紅燒、番茄到麻辣等都有,麵條也巧富變化,各部位肉塊都是靈魂,嚐一碗牛肉麵可說是味覺的多元享受。

時下街邊牛肉麵最常見還是清燉或紅燒,以中藥材熬煮的湯底甚少,位於舊公寓 2 樓的時寓便以此類著稱,多年前一開張便非常受歡迎。

低調的營業樓層多了神秘色彩,棕色木門後是調暗燈光的放鬆氣氛,坐在

時寓
Shiyu
Instagram shiyu.taipei

台北市中山區建國北路一段 68 號 2 樓
02-2506-9209
12:00-14:30, 18:00-22:00(Sat&Sun-21:00)closed on Mon&Tue

老桌老椅裡,牆面掛滿時鐘,此時店小二從蔘茸燕中藥櫃走了出來,記上食客點的麻辣牛肉麵、綜合滷味和梅酒就走進廚房,都令人彷彿掉入不同時光裡。

以數種中藥材與蔬果慢熬細煮,將家傳養身的配方端上麵店餐桌,讓湯中有層次清爽的藥材香與蔬果甜味,喝起來溫潤鮮甜,大把青江菜鋪滿湯碗,配著涮嘴嚼勁的拼盤滷味,熱湯不夠還能加,都像在家一樣,原來時寓讓人一次就上癮,是因為不只賣麵,也賣最好的時光。

Taiwan's beef noodle soup or *niu rou main*, is definitely a must try for anyone visiting the island. The broth varieties are endless, from clear broths to dark ones, tomato broths to hot and spicy - Taiwan's beef noodle flavours are as varied as the noodles themselves. To make things more complex, each cut of beef offers a different texture and sensation, giving every bowl of *niu rou main* a distinctive character.

Nowadays, the most common street food-style beef noodles typically feature clear or dark broths. Very few stores still offer the traditional Chinese herbal broth, and one of the very best stops to find this at, is *Shiyu*. This noodle store, located on the second floor of an old Taipei apartment, caused quite a commotion in the Taipei food scene when it first opened several years ago, both for its authentic vintage interior and for the absolutely lip-smackingly delicious bowl of beef noodle soup!

The low-profile interior is an enigma. Dim lights shine through the window on the brown wooden gate, bringing in slants of light that give the restaurant a soft, calming atmosphere. Antique tables and chairs, old clocks ticking away on the walls, and cabinets well stocked with Chinese herbs behind the counter, make up the scene of an old Taiwanese apartment. Expect spicy beef noodles, *lu wei* (an assorted platter of soy-braised meats and vegetables) and sweet plum wine.

The broth that brings together every bowl of beef noodles is a concoction of Chinese herbs, fruits and vegetables that the owner says is a special family recipe. Every taste of the broth is accompanied with layers of perfectly balanced richness, sweetness

and savouriness. The bright green *pak choi* for garnish, offers some freshness to the thick broth and the *lu wei* platter of tender meats and vegetables, makes for the perfect side dish. If one bowl of soup wasn't enough for you, the staff will happily give you a top up - just like eating at home in the kitchen of a Taiwanese mother. The name of the restaurant, *Shiyu*, can be translated as '*time apartment*' in Chinese, which perfectly encapsulates the homey, carefree ambiance that this venue wonderfully delivers.

路邊屋台小攤起家的阿娥水餃，以老闆娘的名字命名，取得親切樸實也深刻，如同店裡的水餃看起來平凡，滋味卻非常不簡單。每日手工新鮮現包，以招牌的韭黃蝦仁鮮肉水餃收服台北眾人的胃袋。

獨食的點法可以是一份水餃再加上一小碗酸辣湯，水餃以整隻蝦仁、韭黃和豬絞肉入餡，縱使個頭不大，但完美的菜肉比例，飽滿真材實料咬下是鮮美湯汁在嘴中流竄；眾人一同可再多點上幾份小菜，一盒盒包好放在冷藏櫃裡想吃就自己拿，價格清楚標示在菜單上。

阿娥水餃一顆只賣 6 元在台北市區人潮總是絡繹不絕，店家固定週休二日因此只有週間才吃得到。

阿娥水餃
A'e Dumplings

台北市中山區南京東路二段 21 巷 9 樓
02-2571-8628
11:30-19:00 closed on Sat&Sun

A'e Dumplings is named after its owner - the lady who developed what was once a humble street stall into what is now a recognised quality establishment in Taipei. It's cordial, simple and genuine, just like the dumplings that are served by A'e - they might look ordinary, but they definitely taste extraordinary. Each dumpling is handmade daily and stuffed with a generous filling of Asian chives, whole prawns and pork mince in a flavour combination that is set to conquer taste buds in Taipei. They don't look huge, but they have the perfect vegetable-to-meat ratio which never fails to deliver a mouthful of juicy savoury goodness.

If you're dining alone, the perfect combo is to order a single portion of dumplings and a small bowl of hot and sour soup. For social eaters, feel free to take your pick from the myriad of tasty side dishes from the fridge (prices are conveniently marked on the menu), perfect for sharing with friends.

At NT$ 6 each, *A'e's dumplings* are the perfect crowd-pleaser. Be sure to visit during the week as the store closes on weekends.

早餐想吃碗熱熱的魚湯，在台北善導寺站杭州南路一段 11 巷內也有，狹小巷道裡有間總是熱鬧的小攤，由家族經營的以馬內利鮮魚湯已傳至第三代共同經營，40 多年來菜單從沒改過，其中鮮魚湯搭炒米粉（或炒麵）最多人點，兩種主食都想吃就點綜合。

鮮魚湯使用吳郭魚新鮮現煮，清鮮魚湯和細嫩魚肉還入了九層塔葉好鮮好香，自己都等到最後才把九層塔夾進嘴裡，讓清湯多點香氣。雖然魚刺多，但熟客們都知道吐刺時不要墊衛生紙，直接豪邁地往鐵桌上放，待會

以馬內利鮮魚湯
Emmanuel Fish Soup

台北市中正區杭州南路一段 11 巷 3 號對面
02-2351-5378
10:00-18:00（Sat-14:00）closed on Sun

店家好清理。點綜合麵會有麵與米粉各半，炒麵是白麵咬起來扎實有味；炒米粉用的是店家請製麵廠特製的粗米粉，淋上一點油醋與辣椒，更是豐富提味。

每次來都會發現獨食的饕客，點上一碗 80 元的鮮魚湯，再來一份炒麵或炒米粉，幾張桌位所有人並肩擠在一塊，不消 10 幾分鐘的時間就將魚肉與麵條嗑完，靜靜地吃，再靜靜地離開，當桌面堆滿了魚刺代表今日又是愉快滿意的一餐。

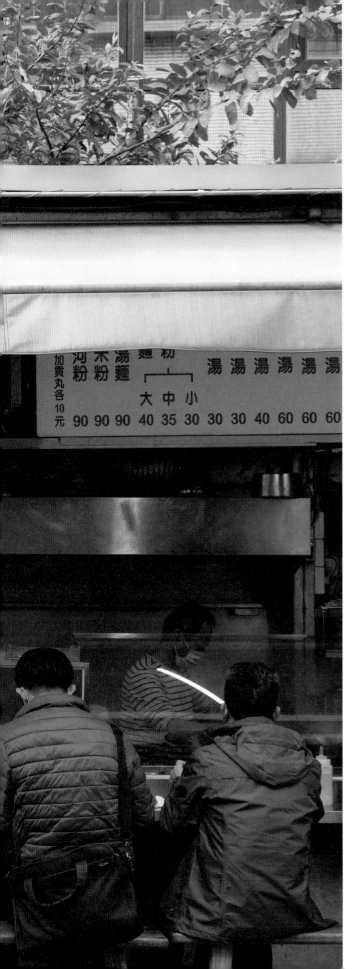

河 不 湯 麵 粉
粉 粉 麵 ⌐┴┐ 湯 湯 湯 湯 湯 湯
加 大 中 小
賣 90 90 90 40 35 30 30 30 40 60 60 60
丸
各
10
元

Located at Lane 11, Section 1, Hangzhou South Road, near Shandao Temple MRT Station, the Emmanuel Fish Soup has been passed down through three generations of hardworking Taiwanese owners. As testament to their skills, their menu has remained exactly the same for more than 40 years and the locals are no stranger to the treasures that the shop outputs - a signature set meal consisting of a hearty bowl of fish soup and stir-fried vermicelli or noodles, or both.

The fish soup is comprised of a clear broth made with fresh tilapia and infused with a hint of Taiwanese basil which adds a noticeable and well-paired fragrance. The roughly chopped chunks of tilapia inside mean that you might be surprised with some fish bones - just pile these on the table as the locals do and the staff will clean them up. The stir-fried noodles have a beautiful springy texture and the slightly thicker than normal vermicelli is sourced from a local mill which has enjoyed a long history with the store. If you're in the mood for an extra kick, spice up your noodles with a splash of vinegar and chilli oil.

When you visit the store, you might find many single eaters sitting side-by-side along the narrow rows of tables, chowing down on their food. After only 10 minutes, you'll see customers leaving, with a satisfied smile on their faces, an empty bowl and a pile of fish bones left on the table.

台北的興波咖啡連續 2 年被國際旅遊網站《Big 7 Travel》評選為「全球 50 間最棒咖啡館」首位，土生土長的興波咖啡將世界冠軍落腳台北，除了網站評選外，創辦人吳則霖也是 2016 年世界咖啡冠軍，從單車咖啡至今日華山文創區旁兩層樓街店的成立，都是咖啡理想的實現。

初訪興波不如先從最純粹的風味開始，試試不定期更換的吳則霖特選批次單品豆，咖啡師以精準的水量、溫度沖煮出迷人的花果香；喜歡有點特別的，那就選融入台灣元素的台灣茶風味拿鐵，濃厚茶香與醇厚咖啡風味相輔相成，達到最舒服且難忘的韻味。

興波咖啡

Simple Kaffa

Instagram simplekaffa

台北市中正區忠孝東路二段 27 號
02-3322-1888
10:00-17:00

嚐過招牌甜點皺皺與抹茶卷後，便每次來都必點。濕潤鬆軟蛋糕體溢著蜂蜜甜香，抹茶卷則是在嘴裡清爽化開透著微甜苦韻，若只為了甜點來也絕不失望。

旗艦店將 2 層樓舊建築重新規劃在空間上有許多令人玩味的細節，大尺度吧檯讓咖啡風味各司其職，品飲區更是多種風格融合，走近 2 樓窗邊彷彿瞬間迎向晴朗自然氣息，來到興波咖啡，是品味咖啡甜食之際，也細品生活建築空間。

Simple Kaffa was ranked the Best 50 Coffee Shops in the World by the *Big Seven Travel* guide not once, but twice. *Simple Kaffa* is the brainchild of Berg Wu, who was crowned champion of the 2016 World Barista competition. What originally started out as a bicycle cart, is now situated within a two-story building located next to the *Huanshan 1914 Creative Park* in Taipei.

During the first visit to *Simple Kaffa*, it's better to start off by tasting Wu's special single-origin beans which constantly change throughout the year. After watching their baristas apply their

half-baked castella cake that will definitely hit the spot. The matcha swiss rolls are deliciously light but deliver a powerful bittersweet hit, while the zhou zhou is a brilliantly moist, soft and infused with the sweet fragrance of honey. If you're not a fan of coffee, *Simple Kaffa* is worth visiting even only just to try their desserts.

Besides coffee and cakes, the building itself is also something to behold. The coffee shop is housed within an old converted building and features a large brewing bar that is equipped with everything a barista needs to produce the best

expertly calibrated amount of water at the perfect temperature, the result is a cup of floral and fruity coffee that is sure to re-ignite your passion for coffee. If you're up for something interesting, check out their lattés which are infused with Taiwanese tea leaves grown right here on the island. The strong tea aromas and the mellow coffee flavours complement each other perfectly to achieve one of the most comforting and unforgettable beverage experiences.

If you've got a sweet tooth, check out their matcha swiss rolls or *zhou zhou* - a *"Hanjuku"* or

cup of coffee for every customer. The windows are large and bold and perfectly match the interior decor to produce a natural and calming ambiance. Each trip to *Simple Kaffa* brings together world-class drinks, luxurious desserts and tasteful architecture and ambiance to give you an unforgettable coffee experience.

Deux Doux crèmerie, pâtisserie & café (以下簡稱 Deux Doux) 像是冰品的展覽室，一年四季都有令人驚艷的作品上桌。主廚 Wilson 於法國雷諾特廚藝學校研習烘焙後不做甜點，回國反倒最先成立義式手工冰淇淋店 Double V，開業至今研發超過 500 種口味，我都說，Wilson 就像是冰的百科全書，好像沒有什麼冰點變化是難得倒他的。

Deux Doux 堅持每季換一次冰單，不只將時令水果與在地食材融入冰點，也佐以甜點元素。像是夏季曾推出的烏龍桃桃，使用淺焙烏龍冰淇淋、白

Deux Doux
crèmerie, pâtisserie & café

Instagram deuxdouxcremerie

台北市松山區長春路 494 號 1 樓
02-8712-8707
12:30-20:00（Last order 19:30）Wed-Fri
12:00-19:30（Last order 19:00）Sat-Sun

桃香檳雪酪、玫瑰白桃雪酪與拉拉山水蜜桃、抹茶酥餅、白巧克力薄片等食材拼湊出清爽宜人的夏季冰點；冬季的葡萄葡萄，則有以新鮮巨峰葡萄做成了雪酪再佐以紫蘇葡萄鑽石冰、夏內多葡萄酒醋雪酪、希臘優格冰淇淋和酒漬櫻桃，是多了些陶醉的溫暖。

在 Deux Doux 不只獲得顛覆味覺的衝擊滿足，如藝術品般的冰點更是視覺享受，也是讓我有了一年四季都想吃冰的幸福理由。

The *Deux Doux Crèmerie, Pâtisserie & Café* (referred to as *Deux Doux*) is like an exhibition for ice cream, always featuring an ever-exciting dazzling array of works and flavours throughout the year. After honing his pastry skills at the *École Lenôtre* in Paris, owner and chef, Wilson Chen returned to Taiwan and established his first store, *Double V*, selling handmade gelato. Since its opening, Wilson's gelateria has exploded into a repertoire of more than 500 flavours. It's not an exaggeration when people refer to Wilson as a walking ice cream encyclopaedia!

The ever-changing menu at *Deux Doux* is seasonal, making good use of fruits and local ingredients in innovative combinations to bring out the best of fine ingredients. In the summer, you can find '*Oolong Peach*' on the menu - a refreshing parfait with an impressive and mouth-watering list of flavours: a light-roasted oolong tea ice cream, white peach champagne sorbet, rose white peach sorbet, Taiwanese peach ice cream, matcha bretonnes and finished with a white chocolate tuille. In contrast, in the winter, Wilson's crafts include a mountain of shaved ice, topped with shiso and famed Japanese kyoho grapes, and a Chardonnay vinegar sorbet served with a Greek yoghurt ice cream and maraschino cherries.

At *Deux Doux*, every dish is a bespoke combination of the finest ingredients blended into innovative gastronomic art, that not only looks and tastes spectacular, but will make you check their menu all year round.

同樣是蔬食料理，針葉林的擺盤繽紛、用料多變、滋味豐饒，甚至調味也拿捏細膩有味，讓平時只願家聚才走進純素餐館的我，偶爾早起就想驅車至木柵，來份無肉早午餐。

靜雅的氛圍也別於過去印象裡的蔬食餐廳，一樓規劃為工作廚房，座席皆設置於 2 樓，細長形的空間有一面寫下日子的木窗，室內悠閒的氣息正好緩緩安撫走過繁忙街道的心緒。早間聽著鍋鏟敲起的清脆聲響，好像家人正料理著早餐，柔和音樂陣陣飄揚，當等待料理人將蔬食豐味端上桌時，也讓自己慵慵懶懶的精神得以轉換釋放。

針葉林

TAIGA

Instagram taigamuzha

台北市文山區木柵路三段 125-1 號
02-2234-2231
09:00-17:00 closed on Mon

幾次來都試了夏威夷照燒三明治，疊上紅卷萵苣、芝麻葉與番茄等層層菜葉，抹上邪惡花生醬料，再配一杯滋味鮮美的柑橘堅果飲，這裡所有的食材皆是料理人每日至鄰近傳統市場採買，再手作製成，讓全素的早餐料理有著更鮮香酸甜真實的味覺體驗，有時一週當中，大概就屬這餐最是純粹。

針葉林是來自有多家連鎖門市「蔬河」另立的品牌，靈感與菜單皆取自店主阿姨一家人在台南的飯桌早餐，各種麵包夾上鷹嘴豆泥等營養蔬果，再採自己庭院種的迷迭香、蘿勒等香草葉裝飾入菜，就成了現在針葉林的模樣。這裏的蔬食做得真好，是會讓你每次來都滿心期待的那種。

Colourful plating, interesting ingredients, developed flavours and precise seasonings - *TAIGA's* well-honed veggie dishes are mind-blowing. Even someone like me who used to avoid walking into a vegetarian spot except for special family reunions, will want to wake up early for a long drive to *Muzha* for one of their must-impress brunches.

With elegance and serenity, *TAIGA* breaks the stereotype of a typical veggie restaurant in Taiwan. The first floor is the kitchen, while the second floor hosts a modest seating area. The tall wooden

every day or are home-grown straight from the owner's garden. All kinds of bread are served alongside delicious hummus and fresh fruits and vegetables. Expect delightful flavours and bright veggie dishes, such as their signature *Hawaiian Teriyaki Sandwich*, topped with lollo rosso lettuce, crisp rocket and succulent tomatoes and finished with a naughty dollop of peanut butter. Finish off the perfect lunch with a glass of refreshing guilt-free marmalade nut milk.

As the sister of the famed franchise *VEGE CREEK*, *TAIGA* is inspired by the breakfast table of the

windows resemble 日, which is the Chinese character for "*day*" or "*sun*". This relaxing restaurant offers solace away from the hustle and bustle of modern life in the city. The distinctive sound of metal spatulas busy in the kitchen, brings to mind a simple breakfast in the comfort of your own home. The dulcet tones of the music playing in the background keep you company while waiting for the food - the definition of a perfect laid-back morning.

On the menu, are dishes crafted from ingredients either sourced meticulously from local markets

owner who moved to Taipei from Tainan. The vegetarian dishes here are so well executed that it will leave you wondering when you'll next visit.

現在回憶起老台北城，反倒時常遺忘了幾十年前與自己好近的七、八〇年代。

有感於此，詹記麻辣火鍋二代詹巽智與夥伴陳米奇兩人特別想將屬於六七年級生的台北日常留在敦南店裡，當時找到了閒置多年曾是台電給員工使用的康樂會館，老舊的建築外觀正好也符合心中想像，有了空間後兩人便開始透過記憶將屬於自己年代的舊時光拼湊。

將麻辣火鍋店設計了華廈入口，有管理員櫃檯、信箱，甚至敞開電梯口，找了開運竹、紫水晶、為數壯觀的鹽燈，也養了紅龍在水族箱，甚至裝上年代久遠的流明天花板，將從前兒時獨有的店家回憶一一搬上場。

詹記麻辣火鍋 敦南店

Chan Chi Hot Pots Lab - Dunnan Branch

台北市大安區和平東路三段 60 號
02-2377-7799
12:00-01:00

「要好玩！」也是兩人對於敦南店的不二初衷。三不五時和藝術家聯名辦展，偶爾心血來潮與設計師合作推出周邊商品，社群平台也經營得有趣，當然不忘本業食物上的創新突破，像是與萬波合作的白菊花茶聯名飲品。

敦南店也承襲創始店 26 年來的老滋味，這裡有台北人津津樂道的麻辣鴨血湯底，是口感扎實滑順且噴香，私心每次來都再必點手工蛋餃和油條，放進鍋裡簡單涮幾秒鐘，酥脆油條包覆著麻辣湯汁，實在好香。

由二代領軍的敦南店吃的是又潮又有態度的懷舊新台味，原來在這麻辣鍋又麻又辣又美味只是輔料，時髦才是當代正統主食。來這也強烈建議訂位，不然很可能會白跑一趟。

Shadowed by these landmarks, the distinctive Taipei style buildings of the 70s and 80s are gradually being forgotten by the younger generation. Aiming to evoke people's memories of the old Taipei town, second-generation owners Chan Chuang Chi and Liu Mi Chi have tried their best to bring back the 70s street scene into their highly respected establishment - the *Chan Chi Hot Pots Lab*.

Transformed from what was originally a sports centre reserved for the employees of the Taiwan Power electricity company, this retro venue perfectly summarises the duo's theme. Their distinguished venue is modelled after the iconic old-school Taiwanese apartment buildings of the 70s, complete with its glass paned entrance, characteristic reception desk, steel mail boxes, cream-coloured lifts and passé but unforgettable decor such as bamboo plants, amethysts and salt lamps. The seating area is illuminated by an ornate array of recognisable mosaic ceiling lights and a large aquarium housing a red arowana - a fierce and proud fish that any Taiwanese will tell you their memories of. These small details come together and bring to life a modern view of old Taiwan.

"*Be quirky and playful*", is the owner's mantra, who frequently invite artists to display their works in the restaurant or work together with local designers and brands, such as the *Wanpo Tea Shop* which brought us their celebrated white chrysanthemum tea.

26 years since its opening, the original branch has been serving traditional hot pot elements such as the silky and flavoursome spicy duck blood cake, signature hand-made egg dumplings and *you tiao* (fried bread stick). A few seconds in the boiling broth and each will quickly soak in the delicious, fragrant and numbing soupy goodness.

There is no doubt that the second-generation owners of this family-run business, have done an exceptionally good job at renewing interest in traditional Taiwanese ambiance for younger, more modern diners. A table at *Chan Chi Hot Pots Lab* is notoriously difficult to secure - be sure to make a reservation well in advance!

自從 BRUSH & GREEN 搬至潮州街後，更多綠意植栽佔據了向陽角落，這裡
便成了我們綠化居家空間與挑禮時最常探訪之處。

當初只因日籍店主東泰利在 61note 將清潔工具隨手一掛，或許是南非手
工製鴕鳥毛撢子太過特別，所以引起客人高度詢問，便誤打誤撞開始了清
潔刷具的生意。

當 61note 的空間再也不足以負荷時，店主便於 2016 年另成立了 BRUSH &

BRUSH & GREEN

Instagram brush_and_green

台北市大安區潮州街 80 號
02-2550-0849
10:30-19:30（Sat-20:30）closed on Mon&Tue

GREEN 專門店，在台北從沒見過整間店擺滿近百款刷具，像是清潔百葉窗
專用、植物葉片細刷、或模樣像刺蝟的鞋底刷等，逛了一圈真是長了不少
知識，原來清潔有如此多細節與學問。

每次來，也留心忘返在一盆盆城市懶人植物前，這裏多以觀葉、文竹、多
肉等好照顧，且不需太多直照的盆栽販售為主，而店主獨特的品味讓店內
坐鎮的植株都特別雅緻，生活感的風格更令每次探訪的心情格外清朗。

After its relocation to *Chaozhou street*, BRUSH & GREEN has blossomed with more greenery and has rooted itself as one of our most frequently visited spots for home decor and gifts for loved ones.

The story of the store began when Mr Yasutoshi Azuma, one day, while cleaning his first store *61note*, unintentionally hung up a feather duster - the duster, handmade from South African ostrich feathers, was so fascinating that it piqued endless questioning from customers. Eventually in 2016, Yasutoshi decided to open *BRUSH & GREEN*. The store's theme is an odd sight in Taipei, stocking over one hundred cleaning-rated products, ranging from those for cleaning blinds, to plant leaves to hedgehog-shaped boot scrapers. Who knew the world of cleaning was this interesting!

In particular, we love coming here to look at their plant range. Specific items that focus on certain foliage such as ferns and succulents make looking after plants much easier - perfect for busy city-dwellers. The owner's aesthetic for selecting beautiful and practical items to stock the shelves is a sight to behold, and we're sure that you'll enjoy the ambiance of the store.

「原來吃一碗冰，能心生幸福況味。」猶記多年前將金雞母的春暖大花玫瑰冰舀到一滴不剩，碗裡原有湯圓、有茶凍、有草莓乾，再淋上自製玫瑰花醬成了朱紅色澤的透涼冰山，那芳醇療癒令人心心念念著。

以綿密鬆軟的日式刨冰結合傳統台式自製配料，像是選用台灣鐵觀音茶製成茶凍，屏東大花農場有機玫瑰花瓣做成淋醬，講究純手工熬煮的真材實料和減糖配方，口味更輕盈清爽了，也照顧現代人想吃冰，卻又在意吃進太多熱量的矛盾心情。

金雞母

Jingimoo

Instagram jingimoo

台北市中正區杭州南路一段 143 巷 36 號
0908-232-108
12:30-20:30

I still remember the first time I tried the "*Spring Blossom Rose Shaved Ice*" from *Jingimoo* three years ago - a poppy-red mountain of shaved ice, topped with Hakka-style mochi balls, tea flavoured agar jelly, dried strawberries and homemade rose jam. When it arrived, the air was filled with the fragrance of refreshing strawberries and immediately I was awash with the sensation of happiness and tranquillity.

Jingimoo cleverly fuses together Japanese shaved ice with Taiwanese toppings into a delightful explosion of flavour in every bite. Expect a speciality menu featuring their refreshing tea-flavoured agar made from Taiwanese tieguanyin oolong tea and gems such as organic rose petal jam, all sourced from fresh local ingredients. On top of that, *Jingimoo* places special emphasis on low-sugar recipes, offering sweet-toothed diners a guilt-free way of getting their fill.

古宅水泥牆上布著青苔，不規則的石塊幾許剝落，木門不再花樣青澀而是有了歲月痕跡，推開香色斑駁墨綠門後，時光彷彿是停留在歐洲中古世紀。

打扮麻質衣裳的香色朋友引領我們入座，一盞盞燭燈，是記錄下當時空氣裡的歡樂，偶爾望向外頭那整片翁鬱天空，彷彿與世隔絕般度過。

在台北，重要日子想好好紀念時，還好總是還有香色。與重要的人聚在一塊，你我稍微認真打扮圍坐著，這裡週間開放晚餐料理，假日則還有供應輕食早午餐，任何時候來，都有主廚用盡心思的創意菜餚，在閃耀的燭光下，留下最美好的片刻。

香色

Xiang Se

Instagram xiangse

台北市中正區湖口街 1-2 號
02-2358-1819
Tue-Thu 17:30-22:00 / Fri 17:30-22:30
Sat 11:30-15:30, 17:30-22:30
Sun 11:30-15:30, 17:30-22:00

Old concrete walls habituated with moss, irregular rocks mottled with age and a set of hefty green doors, unshy to show its years. Push open the door and step into the courtyard where you'll be greeted by the familiarity of Europe.

Welcome to *Xiang Se*, undoubtedly one of the best and most reliable spots in Taipei when in need of a presentable and unforgettable dining experience to celebrate those special events that life throws in one's way.

The kitchen is open for dinner on weekdays, but only offers a brunch service on weekends. Every time you visit *Xiang Se*, you experience a part of the chef's thoughts, which under the candlelight, helps create some of the most cherishable memories.

最喜歡 Ruins Coffee Roasters 那走上窄梯的小閣樓，大家圍坐一起溫馨的氣氛，也特別寫意，坐在上頭總會忍不住往下四處張望，好奇接著玻璃門敞開又是誰走了進來，也好奇咖啡師下一秒將變出什麼療癒咖啡。

Ruins Coffee Roasters 的成立說來話長，不過簡短來說，這裏最早是主理人開開烘豆的場地，因位於河堤旁通風不怕干擾到左鄰右舍，接著老頑童咖啡師駐點企劃讓此地活絡起來，後來才因市中心的小破爛結束營業，2017 年便決定在此地以 Ruins Coffee Roasters 重新開始。

店內義式手沖都有，主攻自家淺焙豆，也能嚐到中深焙的豆子。菜單上還

Ruins Coffee Roasters

Instagram ruinscoffeeroasters

台北市文山區木柵路三段 242 號
02-2234-0024
13:00-21:00 closed on Mon

有一款相當特別的飲品，是來自已歇業的 20 多年老店「一席」流下的秋日冰咖啡，一席為了讓喜歡的熟客們未來皆能再嚐到那記憶裡的滋味，結束營業時便將店內 20 幾款飲品一一傳授至不同的咖啡館。

得到的秋日冰咖啡以深焙濃縮為基底，藏著隱約的桂花香氣，香甜醇厚的咖啡味是不喝咖啡的人也會喜歡，而喜歡喝咖啡的則是會愛上那風味。

現在的 Ruins Coffee Roasters 由開開負責店內營運與咖啡烘焙，姊姊則負責甜點，也加入了新夥伴，小小的廢墟，像是裝滿了最溫暖美好的簡單生活。

Walking up narrow stairs into the small attic where you find *Ruins Coffee Roasters* is always an exciting start to something nice. The homey and cosy space is perfect for sitting in, watching the coming and going of visitors and the baristas busy at work with their creations.

The story of how *Ruins Coffee Roasters* came to be is a long and interesting one. But in a nutshell, it was originally opened as a roastery situated along the riverside, picked for its good ventilation and quiet location that minimised the chance of disturbing the neighbours. The roastery quickly became lively, but eventually relocated to the current site in 2017 due to size issues.

Ruins offers espresso-style coffees, pour overs and their special Autumn cold brew coffee which was famously served at the *Yi Shi coffee house* which closed its doors more than a decade ago. Luckily, *Yi Shi* made available the brewing recipes to some twenty of their most popular beverages to different bars across the city, allowing us the chance to revel in a part of Taipei's coffee history.

Ruins places their focus on light-roast varieties, but medium and dark roasts are also available and are excellent options for those not a fan of fruity acidity. Currently, the roastery is run by Kai Kai, who manages the cafe and roastery's daily operations, while her sister is in charge of the baked goods that serve as a perfect accompaniment to your coffee. *Ruins Coffee Roasters* is simply a must visit cafe for any urban dweller.

來自礁溪的白水豆花生意真好，幾乎每次路過都有人在排隊，不過若你選擇戶外吃，通常不消幾分鐘就能排到。

這裡豆花有粉圓與桃膠兩種口味可選，彈滑質地濃郁豆香的鹽滷豆花，均搭配細口甜味的花生糖粉與香菜，據說店主當初佐料的靈感，卽是來自礁溪花生捲冰淇淋名店，入了香菜著實畫龍點睛，那鮮香也豐富了口感甜味，而兩種口味自己則偏愛軟Q滑嫩的粉圓更多。

店鋪外總能見食客捧著立食的情景，每回都令我聯想起西門町阿宗麵線的盛況，只不過這裡有綠意包圍，也能端至公園坐下慢嚐，怎樣都愜意地多！

白水豆花

Bai Shui Tofu Pudding

Instagram baishuidouhua

台北市大安區永康街 31 巷 9 號 1 樓
02-2392-6707
14:00-21:00 closed on Thu

Business at *Bai Shi Tofu Pudding* from *Jiaoxi* is really good. It seems like every time you pass by, there's always a long queue, but if you only order to eat outside, it usually takes less than a few minutes.

Bai Shui's dou hua (tofu pudding) comes with a choice of two toppings: tapioca boba or peach resin. The *dou hua*'s salty creamy texture with a rich aroma of soybeans is paired with a sweet peanut powder and fresh crisp coriander. The choice of these condiments were inspired by *Jiaoxi's* famous peanut ice cream rolls. The coriander is really an exceptional finishing touch, as it leaves every bite with a crisp, refreshing sweetness.

Outside the store, are always groups of customers standing around, enjoying their *dou hua*. The sight reminds me of the noodles from *Ah Zong's Vermicelli* in *Ximending*. A similar sight, the store is surrounded by greenery and there is a park nearby where you can take your freshly purchased noodles to sit down to enjoy.

很難想像在台北還能有像寶藏巖聚落這樣一個地方，倚著山坡而立的屋舍，為現在居民在過去搬著一磚一瓦徒手而建，如今蜿蜒步道而上藏著許多寶藏，是一間間裝載藝文與料理的空間。其中尖蚪算是「寶藏巖國際藝術村」聚落共生元老級的經營者，除了規劃有趣的藝文活動外，平日則有提供旅人與藝術家的餐食。

非餐飲科系出身的主理人小嬉手藝裡注入了溫暖的家常感。招牌的飯團捏得真好，光是紫蘇的鮮美香氣就令人入口生津，再附上自漬梅乾添上豐富

尖蚪
Tadpole Point Cafe
Instagram tadpole.point

台北市中正區汀州路三段 230 巷 57 號
02-2369-2050
13:00-20:00（Sat&Sun 11:00-20:00）closed on Mon&Tue

酸甜；像是溫潤爽口的胡麻豆腐；還有來自深夜食堂的貓飯在餐桌上不停的飄動，一顆半熟蛋、一點醬汁就是最生動有味的餐飯；另外多了酸勁的抹茶冰茶，與藏著獨特香氣的尖蚪鮮奶茶都好。

中午開始陽光從 2 樓的窗口探進頭來，微風也徐徐而來，嚐著美味飯菜同時，也讓人體會像山中的簡單自在。

It's hard to imagine that a place like the *Treasure Hill Artist Village* exists in central Taipei. What was originally an old scenic village built into the hillside that housed military veterans, is now home to cafes and boutiques which somehow resonate with the name of the village - a hill of hidden treasures. The oldest story of the village can be told by the *Tadpole Point Café* which has for a long time been serving hearty food to locals and visitors alike. The café also holds art events which attracts artists from all over the country.

Hsiao Hsi, the owner, is not a cook - the food served here is humble but homey and delicious. The signature *onigiri*, a Japanese-style rice ball, contains home-pickled *umeboshi* (Japanese pickled plums), parcelled in a vibrant leaf of *shiso*. Their tofu salad is topped with a savoury and well-balanced Japanese sesame dressing that is as comforting as it is delicious. The most famous dish here is the '*neko manma*' or '*rice for cats*' that was made famous by the Japanese TV series '*Midnight Diner*'. The *neko manma* is a bowl of sushi rice, topped with a poached egg, a soy sauce dressing and bonito flakes that appear to whimsically dance to the rising steam of the rice. The café also serves a selection of homemade beverages including a matcha lemon iced tea and a special house milk tea which is sure to quench your thirst.

During the afternoon, sitting upstairs on the second floor, with the sunlight beaming through the window, accompanied by the cool breeze and the smell of comforting cuisine, will lull you into thinking that you're at a mountain resort.

宜人的中山區商圈裡有處眾人皆知的世外桃源，怎說呢？已開業 10 年的 61note，算是國內外生活期刊入鏡的常客，很多人就算從未造訪也必知其名號；不太醒目的綠意轉角像是刻意低調著，卻也讓整間店別有一番悠閒舒心圍繞。

日本限定的帆布包是特點，地下一樓有一整層日籍店主東泰利先生獨家代理的帆布包品牌 TEMBEA，Made in Japan 是在設計、功能與材質細節都照顧得很好，因應各式需求的包款應有盡有，自己人生第一個裝法式長棍帆布包 (Baguette Tote) 也是在此購入的。

不只限定選物，一樓啤酒餐食吧也好適合與朋友各自點杯台味微醺酒精，再嚐份蕃茄濃郁酸辣香氣的日式咖哩飯，度過台日家常的慢慢味道。

61 note

61note.com.tw
Instagram 61note

台北市大同區南京西路 64 巷 10 弄 6 號
02-2550-5950
12:00-21:00 closed on Mon

There are many hidden gems around the hipster *Zhongshan* area and *61note* is one of them. A frequent name seen on foreign lifestyle magazines, *61note* has gained a reputation, both locally and internationally. Its understated appearance, with sprawling greenery, effortlessly commands an aura of relaxation.

Limited edition Japanese canvas bags are the calling card of *61note*. In the basement, you'll find a proud display of the TEMBEA collection - a Japanese label that made its way into Taiwan through *61note's* founder, Mr Yasutoshi Azuma. Each TEMBEA piece is crafted with high quality materials and attention is given to every detail. The selection entails a good variety of bag types. For instance, I bought my first baguette tote from here.

The first floor of the boutique also serves beer from local independent breweries and great food to snack along with it. Devotees will come back time and time again for their signature hot and sour tomato Japanese curry.

61NOTE

COFFEE · BEER · SELECT SHOP

61 BEER

61NOTE
SHOP & TEA

No.6, Aly. 10, Ln. 64
Nanjing W. Rd., Datong Dist.

Tel:02-2550-5950

Tue-Thu, Sun 12:00~21:00

Monday closed

1F Shop & Tea
B1 Gallery

位於城西的 MKCR 有著得天獨厚的地理位置，這裏前方是寬闊的廣場，二樓窗邊能與歷史古蹟北門對望，窗外城市流動如畫更盡收眼底，不遠交通轉運樞紐也讓此地成為外國旅人的必訪之地。

來過 MKCR 好幾次了，小而清新的空間每次午後來都必定座無虛席，該是整日最熱鬧繁忙的時刻。然而自己最鍾情的，還是屬清早的 MKCR，時常只有客人兩三位，你可以專心埋首電腦工作，也能將此地當作旅程起點，補充點咖啡因就前往下一站，坐在靠窗的位子，倚著外頭剛甦醒的那份朝氣，總不自覺地將心情放鬆下來。

來這裡習慣點上招牌的焦糖蘋果生乳酪蛋糕，使用新鮮蘋果肉入餡，是香甜清爽滋味；再佐上濃厚咖啡風味的拿鐵，絕對是城市旅人一日開始的幸福儀式。

MKCR

Instagram mkcrtw

台北市中正區忠孝西路一段 126 號
2-2381-0682
08:00-22:00

MKCR is located in western Taipei, overlooking a spacious square with its second-floor windows affording a beautiful view of the historic North Gate. Due to its proximity to Taipei's transportation hub, it has also become one of the most visited sites for tourists.

Afternoons are the busiest time for MKCR, so as frequent visitors, we prefer the morning hours when you can work cosily with a laptop while getting to know your morning coffee. Sitting by the windows always boosts our mood and productivity. The house specialty is a caramel apple cheesecake which is infused with refreshing and tart apples. Why not pair yours with a strong latté to kickstart your day?

「等待滴滴點點而下的咖啡汁液，那分秒而過的不經意，在咖啡香氣瀰漫滿室彷彿是種儀式，時空正在奇幻轉換著，我們沉浸那最絢麗的停止，留在與城市迥然不同的光景。」藏身大稻埕裡的幻猻家珈琲，像是一場時光旅行。

主攻咖啡，卻反因咖哩飯與布丁名聞整座台北城市，不過一嚐那細煮慢燉的咖哩，便也明白了，那溫厚的暖是與心好近，肉塊米飯福神漬也好，都是最厚實的滿足；舀一口布丁，像是被家人擁抱最揪心的照顧，不想忘記。

可能是咖哩飯與布丁樣子比較討喜，不然這裏的咖啡其實也甚好，咖啡師慢裡悠閒點滴式出一杯單品，深焙溫和的苦醇，尾韻甘甜悠久繚繞於心。

幻猻家珈琲像是被施了魔法的老屋，那種著迷是使人逃離現實，在這暖暖的生活情境，什麼時候來都很好。

幻猻家珈琲
Pallas Café
Instagram pallascafe

台北市大同區迪化街一段 14 巷 14 號
02-2555-6680
Wed 12:00-18:00 Thu-Sun 10:00-21:00 close on Mon&Tue

The *Pallas Café*, as its name unambiguously suggests, serves coffee. What you might not expect however, is that they're also unconventionally famous for their Japanese curry and caramel puddings. You'll understand why, once you try their slow-cooked curry, paired with the delightful fruity crunch of *fukujinzuke* - a type of pickled vegetables that are commonly used as a relish for Japanese curry. As for the coffee? Expect well-honed pour overs made from a selection of light to dark beans roasted on site.

Like an old apartment alive with magic, the *Pallas Café* encapsulates a sense of escapism, offering a comforting and warm refuge for every one of its visitors.

台北可愛之處，在於地方雖小，卻能廣納各國飲食文化。就算沒去過俄羅斯，也總能在城裡覓得道地的俄國餐點，就像明星咖啡館裡有俄羅斯皇室早年留下食譜的沙皇羅宋湯、俄羅斯魚凍和軟糖等料理，那歷經一甲子的滋味，也將舊時代藝文一同寫下，是格外彌足珍貴的。

曾歷經停業與浴火的明星咖啡館就算多次改裝，至今仍沿用開業時的古董桌椅，汰換多次皮墊的木椅還捨不得丟棄，老派的風格實在太寫意，在這用餐的片刻，總會讓人想像三毛、黃春明、白先勇等人在此執筆寫作的模樣，而後誕生一部部後人廣為流傳的作品。

明星咖啡館

Café Astoria

astoria.com.tw
Instagram astoria1949

台北市中正區武昌街一段 5 號 2 樓
02-2381-5589
10:30-21:30

館裡細緻的味覺享受，也令人魂牽夢縈，招牌沙皇羅宋湯是酸酸甜甜燉滿了料，費時熬煮的魚凍口感鮮香，吃飽了，就再來一杯虹吸咖啡，也搭一塊以桂圓、核桃、葡萄乾製成的明星核桃糕，是不愛吃糕餅類甜食的我，也想再多嚐一塊。

這也難怪過去個個文人都要至此創作，我想或許也是食物讓他們文思泉湧，原來咖啡館不只是常日裡的味蕾陪伴，說是孕育知識且思想激盪的場所，也不為過啊。

One of the most captivating features of Taipei is the diversity in its cultural scene. *Café Astoria* is perhaps one of the best examples as an establishment offering authentic Russian cuisine. Rooted in the lineage of the Russian royal family, its menu features well known classic Russian dishes such as *Beef Borscht, Fish Jelly* and sweet treats such as *Soft Candy*. The restaurant's recipe book includes a staggering 60 years of Russian flavours and has become a timeless and precious heritage of the city.

After briefly shutting its doors in 1989 and then again in 2003 due to a fire, the interior design and furnishing of *Café Astoria* still remains faithful to the original vintage style sported since its first opening. The wooden chairs have had only their leather cushions renewed, but the frames, aged with time, have been left alone to ferment a mature style throughout the restaurant. *Café Astoria* was also famously frequented by some of the literary giants of Taiwan, including San Mao, Huang Chun-Ming and Pai Hsien-Yung - with a pen in one hand and a coffee in the other, in the middle of shaping some of Taiwan's literary masterpieces.

The special atmosphere radiated by *Café Astoria* and its catalogue of delicacies, attract lovers of both literature and the arts - it's no wonder that this restaurant has been recognised as one of the most unique cultural salons in Taipei. *Café Astoria* is not just a restaurant, but a cradle for fostering imaginative and creative works of art.

「我要一杯冰的輕美式。」「在這邊喝。」原來還有這樣特別的選擇，想要濃縮減半就點菜單上「輕」字頭的選項！

很快！玻璃杯裡裝滿酒紅透涼的咖啡香，抹著油脂泡沫的冰塊浮在上頭總是看起來舒暢，接過咖啡後，我們就在鏡頭外對街的長板凳坐下，這裏自成街上時髦的戶外吧，每個人都很有默契地喝完就趕緊起身離開，將杯子遞還給店家。

位於松江路巷弄轉角的夏野豆行，中午總是特別熱鬧，是鄰近上班族因午休無法久待在咖啡店內細細慢品，就會來這帶一份獨特的風味走。

夏野豆行

Summer Savage Coffee

Instagram summersavage2017

台北市中山區松江路 330 巷 1 號
02-2563-8780
08:00-19:00（Sat 10:00-）closed on Sun

Not a fan of that much caffeine? Simply add the word 'light' on your order and your americano will be adjusted to a single shot. After ordering our coffee, we relocated ourselves to the benches across the road from the store. There is no better feeling than that of sipping on a glass of burgundy-brown coffee, topped with a crisp and refreshing layer of buoyant ice cubes. After finishing it, we returned our glass back to the store. Such an urban feeling.

Perhaps because of its proximity to many offices nearby, *Summer Savage* coffeehouse located at the corner of *Songjiang Road* is always sprawling with activity during lunch hours.

台北的選物店不少，卻鮮少有像 A Design&Life Project 這樣，可能正好位於舊城大稻埕的關係，也可能是老房子的氣息使然，一股獨特的台式精神，總之，物件也是特別有味道的。

當初 Shibo 和 Small 兩人只是為了能讓顧客摸到品牌第一款自製包包的質感，就毅然決然開了實體門店，默默的，自己設計開發生產的產品越來越多，目前品牌有近六成都是獨立自產的商品。

喜歡什麼，就去做什麼。從品牌剛成立的包包、玻璃器皿，到還有名為男子漢的收納箱，都是龜毛一點、講究一點、細節一點，才有了現在店裡每一個物件上架亮相，就連空間裡用來陳列商品的木櫃，或照明的燈具，也是別具心意的存在。每次來這，總感覺能挖到許多用心生活的寶物。

A Design&Life Project

adesignandlifeproject.com
Instagram designandlife

台北市大同區南京西路 279 號
02-2555-9908
11:00-19:00

Taipei has no shortage of boutiques, but there are few like *A Design&Life Project*. Perhaps it's because its located within *Dadaocheng* in the old city, or maybe it's because of the atmosphere radiated from the old flats. Either way, it definitely has a unique tasteful Taiwanese feeling to it.

A Design&Life Project came about when co-founders Shibo and Small decided to open a physical store so that customers would be able to touch and feel their first homemade bags. Gradually, more and more products, designed by the duo, filled the shelves. At present, around 60% of the store's inventory are homemade designs. This boutique stocks everything from bags to glassware, to lighting fixtures and larger furniture - every item is placed meticulously on shelves and poised around the store to show off their best features. But more interesting perhaps, is their signature storage box called '*The Man*', folded from galvanized steel and comes in three styles - *silver, hole* or *caramel*.

Attention is paid to every detail of every design, which perfectly encapsulates the unwavering perfectionistic attitude of the duo. Every time I visit this store, I wonder what I'll end up taking home.

20 D&L 15
HARDWARE
& TRADING CO.
PARTS — RETRO — BRASS
RIVERSIDE DAIRY

時隔多日再來，HERE & THERE 已不再是每週固定營業的甜點店了。這裡漸漸更像是店主 Angela 理想的生活模樣，採預約制每月月初於官方平台公告可預約日，通常 1 個月只開放 4 到 5 天，其餘日子想要忙著烘焙甜點；想要分享有趣的手作課、繪畫課；也想要忙著過著喜歡的生活。

而這裏的手作點心也與外頭滋味不同，Angela 稍微變化的配方，讓栗子瑪德蓮嚐著有種古早味雞蛋糕，口感與滋味都好溫柔；而提拉米蘇也稍微改了作法，嚐起來也更過癮。

會這麼喜歡這裡，還有那靜雅的明亮氛圍，一扇扇窗子成了畫框，街上過去年代的古老建築正好成了一幅幅最美的時光寫照，也是大稻埕裡二樓獨有的老城景色。

HERE & THERE

Instagram h_e_r_e_and_t_h_e_r_e

台北市大同區延平北路二段 62 號

reservation only

Once a dessert parlour that had regular opening hours, *HERE & THERE* has slowly turned into a reservation-only cafe that perfectly fits owner Angela's ideal lifestyle and schedule. Bookings can only be made at the beginning of each month upon the announcement of new slots. If that wasn't exclusive enough, *HERE & THERE* is only open four to five days a month. The rest of the time, Angela prefers saving for other hobbies such as drawing and crafts and working through life at her own pace.

The handcrafted desserts here are different from anywhere else. A specialty of *HERE & THERE* is Angela's chestnut madeleine which she has finetuned the flavour to resemble that of a traditional Taiwanese eggy pancake - even replicating its gentle texture and unmistakable taste. The tiramisu is another recipe that has been carefully tweaked.

HERE & THERE is a favourite of mine. The row of bright windows are like picture frames, capturing a picturesque view of the modest row of old-style *Dadaocheng* buildings outside, resonating with the quiet atmosphere of the interior.

曾經多次一早就出現在城西的西門町，做什麼呢？是到蜂大咖啡裡吃份舊時光的早餐。老牌咖啡館裡的火腿蛋吐司可不像街邊早餐店那樣把料層層疊起，這裡的 2 顆太陽蛋煎得大如餐盤，與擺上的三角火腿片，乍看還真像是一張笑臉，另外微烤的吐司抹上鮮紅草莓醬，這樣簡單的組合最適合剛甦醒的身心味蕾了。

隨餐附贈的黑咖啡也不馬虎，輕啜一口即是醇厚豐香於鼻喉間幽幽流轉，是與方才入口的香甜綿柔交織，畢竟這裡本業是賣了 60 幾年的咖啡，店內雖有明定 60 分鐘用餐時間，但足以慢慢品嚐。

離開前，習慣再外帶幾塊核桃酥餅走，接著慢步至武昌街看場電影，成了追憶喜歡的西門時光。

蜂大咖啡

Fong Da Coffee

Facebook 蜂大咖啡

台北市萬華區成都路 42 號
02-2331-6110
08:00-22:00

On many occasions, I have found myself spending my morning in *Ximending* located in the west of the city. What was I doing? Of course I was there for a breakfast at *Fong Da Coffee!*

The ham and egg toast served by this old establishment is not simply layered together like any other street breakfast store. Instead, two sun eggs are fried up and are huge enough to eclipse the dinner plate, with triangular ham slices layered on top. Resembling a smiling face, the egg and ham is served with two slices of thick toast, with a generous glob of strawberry jam on top - flavours that are perfect for a mind that has just woken up.

Don't forget the black coffee that is served with the breakfast. Each sip reveals a mellow and rich flavour that wakes up the olfactory senses. *Fong Da Coffee* hasn't been open for sixty years for no reason! Because of its popularity, the café requires its table back after an hour, but this is plenty of time to enjoy your breakfast at a leisurely pace.

Each time I visited, I used to always pick up some of their walnut shortbread to take away, and then venture towards *Wuchang street* for a movie - my favourite way of spending time in *Ximen*.

「雖名為『東一排骨』，但我現在都點雞腿飯。」會這麼說，其實不是東一的排骨比不上雞腿，而是雞腿飯也很出色，點了 10 幾年的排骨飯偶爾總會吃膩想換口味，那麼這裡還有雞腿飯可以選。

第一次點排骨飯後初期就沒有再換過，先醃半小時再炸的排肉滿溢著層次香氣，爽快嚼勁新鮮粗獷，後來好奇試了雞腿飯，先滷再炸是薄酥外皮咬開，腿肉豐腴帶汁，搭著飯菜一起叫人回味無窮。

光是如此已超級滿足，卻還有老闆娘親手做的湯品，喝過味噌湯、紫菜湯，最特別是用了薑絲、白木耳、大骨一起熬煮的竹筍湯，這裡湯和副菜時常變換，因此就算天天來也總是期待，小菜最推油豆腐，淋上特調的五味醬讓軟嫩豆腐吸附蒜頭、辣椒、豆豉醬油那辛甜鹹味，豐富的汁香，不鹹不膩有味清爽，最是好吃。

東一排骨
Dong Yi Pork Ribs

台北市中正區延平南路 61 號 2 樓
02-2381-1487
10:00-20:00 closed on Mon

已走過半百的東一排骨，是台灣五、六〇年代流行的紅包場、卡啦 OK 風格，風水古物鋼琴一行排開，更有意思地將鮮果吧台裝進餐廳裡，想點水果盤、果汁、咖啡和啤酒都行。

送餐大哥說兩層樓面至少有 300 張席位，用餐時段人再多都不必擔心要等位。在這吃飯絕不無聊，東看西望懷舊新奇，多台液晶電視擺在各個角度，記得聖誕節時也有應景的裝飾與歌曲。

50 年來品質不變的東一排骨，目前交由二代少爺經營，一代老闆娘則在一旁幫忙，服務生感覺清一色都是有歲數的大哥大姐了，那認真親切的氛圍如見台北當年台式料理店的熱鬧模樣。

"*Although the restaurant is most famous for its namesake - pork chops, our pick is their fried chicken leg bento*". Don't get me wrong, it's not that the pork chop bento from *Dong Yi's* is not as good as their chicken leg bento, but the juicy and crispy chicken leg is honestly nearly unbeatable. Anyhow, many of the patrons who have been dining here for decades, love switching between the two versions.

Pork chops at *Dong Yi's* are marinaded for half an hour before deep frying to amp up their flavour. As for our favourite chicken legs, they're thoroughly braised in a soy-based stock, dipped into a thin

drizzle of their special sauce consisting of garlic, chilli and *doubanjiang* (fermented soybean paste) and soy sauce.

Inside *Dong Yi*, you can find everything that represents a Taiwanese establishment in the 1950s and 60s - cabaret, karaoke, Feng Shui antiques, a piano and a juice bar that serves fruit platters, beverages and alcohol. When I asked, the staff told me that there are at least 300 seats across the two floors! Dining here is never boring - there's always interesting to look at depending on where you sit in the restaurant - vintage items, TVs and even apt decorations and background music during

layer of batter, and deep fried to lock in the juicy goodness. Each bite is accompanied by an explosion of juices and meat so satisfyingly tender, that even the first bite will leave you thinking about ordering another. Both the chicken leg and pork chops are served on a bed of perfectly fluffy rice and fresh greens to soak up the juices.

Besides the main dish, each set meal also includes a soup and a side dish which changes every day. Soups range from miso soup, seaweed soup and a bamboo shoot soup with stewed pork marrow, ginger and fungus. For the side dishes, our pick is the deep fried soy-braised tofu served with a

Christmas.

One thing that doesn't change however is the quality of the food produced by *Dong Yi*, which has remained exceptional for more than 50 years. The restaurant is now run by the second generation of the family but the parents still enjoy keeping on the side to offer help. The middle-aged waiters have been working here for a long time, and you can always see them chatting with the regulars, producing a very warm and welcoming dining experience.

每每在大稻埕肚子餓不知道要吃什麼時，就會走往永樂市場旁的金仙魚丸，挑一張空位坐下，有時排骨飯、有時雞腿或蝦捲飯，再配一碗羹湯，就能心滿意足地大快朵頤起來。

牆上菜單幾乎每樣都曾點過，最常吃的還是排骨飯，除了排骨扎實滷香鹹氣很是下飯外，還送一條Q嫩甜香蝦捲，然後一定要沾牛頭牌芥末醬更有滋味；再來就是配菜了，這裡每天固定會有新鮮高麗菜與綠菜，其他副菜則天天更換，有時是炒冬粉，有時是炒瓜，是比城裡其它有些同為金仙名號料理店使用醃菜多一份鮮味外，也更富變化。

金仙魚丸
Jin Shien Fish Balls

台北市大同區南京西路 233 巷 19 號
02-2559-4392
07:00-20:00 closed on Wed

看著滷檯前的大姐拿著長柄鐵匙在鍋裡不停動作，從早上7點至晚餐沒有空班，人潮絡繹不絕生意可真好啊，不過這裡翻桌也快，許多人吃完就走因此通常不須等太久。聽金仙魚丸裡的曾大哥說，大稻埕這間是目前所有金仙開張最久的店，走過30幾個年頭，當初兄弟姐妹們出來以金仙各自為鎮，所以每家作法不同，想想，金仙也能說是台北人從小到大美好的便當記憶了。

Whenever I'm hungry and out of ideas for what to eat in *Dadaocheng* area, I'll pop down to *Jin Shien Fish Balls*, next to the *Yongle market*, where I'll be sure to find something delicious. At *Jin Shien*, you'll get a bowl of rice with different options of proteins including pork ribs, fried chicken legs and fried prawn rolls. Pair that with a bowl of thick Taiwanese soup to perfectly satisfy your stomach.

After trying nearly everything on their menu, we think the definite must try is the pork chop served with a bowl of rice. In addition with the tender and savoury pork chop that is excellent with the fluffy

into the evening. Mr Tseng from *Jin Shien* told me that his siblings eventually opened up their own restaurants, each using the name '*Jin Shien*' - a homage to the name of the small town where they grew up. This *Jin Shien* in *Dadaocheng* however is the oldest, having served simple yet hearty comfort food to the local community for over 30 years. At every *Jin Shien*, you'll find each sibling's version of the same familiar menu. This network of family-run restaurants has undoubtedly become one of the best food memories of people in Taipei.

rice, the meal set also comes served with chewy prawn rolls (be sure to try it with the Colman's mustard) and fresh seasonal Taiwanese greens. Other side dishes to enjoy are the stir-fried mung bean noodles, or their pickled winter melon. Compared to other restaurants that offer their take on the same pickled winter melon, *Jin Shien's* is definitely the most delicious and authentic version.

At *Jin Shien*, you'll find an open kitchen who's chef is a lady that is constantly delivering set after set of delicious meals from 7am until late

尚未實際造訪角公園咖啡之前，總以為這裡與城中其他老房咖啡館並無二異，來了之後你會驚覺這裡的一切，是與日子一同生長的。

各個角落留下兩位店主訴說生活的樣貌，婚姻平權的杯子、「沒有人是局外人」的海報、小白通訊期刊閱讀著音樂、兒童繪本重返童年、郭秋燕的舞拾畫展、大吉大利喜氣春聯、想起青春的音樂卡帶、舒國治的《水城臺北》、十一夜領養不棄養布掛，垂吊的盞盞黃燈從白日亮至黑夜，彷彿都是對生命的種種執著與念頭。

角公園咖啡
Triangle Garden Cafe
Instagram trianglegardencafe

台北市大同區太原路 131 號 2 樓
02-2556-1773
10:00-18:00 (Sat&Sun-21:00)

挑高閣樓二樓，幾乎保留百年老屋最原始的模樣，甚至留下牆上的歲月斑駁，獨一無二的桌椅也似有自己的身世般，光是空間已令人百般陶醉了。來這推薦取名為角公園咖啡的冰飲，是以咖啡冰磚注入牛奶自行調配比例的咖啡牛奶，那是經過時間沉澱而變化的咖啡風味。

已成立 5 年多的角公園咖啡時常客滿，建議想來能先訂位。這裡不限時，總有日光陪伴，雖店名其實另有涵義，但的確也像是街角的公園，愜意舒適。

Until I visited the *Triangle Garden Café*, I always thought that the place was no different than the other many vintage-style cafes in the city, but after I visited, I was surprised at how well the café represented the modern transformation of Taiwanese society.

Everything that you find in the store was placed there as if some profound lesson from the owners teaching us not to forsake our history. A cup printed with the words "*marriage equality*" brings to mind the same-sex marriage referendum of 2019. A poster that features the words "*no one is an outsider*" reminds us about the land rights of Taiwanese indigenous communities. A newsletter from *White Wabbit* - a well known and leading Taiwanese indie music label. A selection of books suitable for all ages, even children. Paintings from the artist Guo Qiuyan. Spring couplets inviting in the Lunar New Year. Music cassettes that are sure to trigger nostalgia. Shu Guozhi's essay *Hsui Cheng Taipei*. A fabric banner speaking out against pet abandonment from the documentary *Eleven Nights*. These items remind the Taiwanese people of not only their history, but their cultural identity and how their society transformed into the one that currently lives with them on the island today.

The old-fashioned bulbs hanging overhead give off a warm yellow light, reverberating with wise and dignified tenure of the store. On the second floor is an attic which perfectly retains the appearance of a century-old Taiwanese house. Every table and chair, wisened by time, seems to have its own story to tell.

Having opened for five years, the *Triangle Garden Café* is popular among locals and visitors alike and so reservations are highly recommended although there's no time limit once you're seated. Their specialty beverage is named after the store - the *Jiao Coffee*, which features an iced glass of milk with cubes of frozen coffee. In Chinese, the name of the café actually means "*the park at the street corner*" which envisions a

serene and tranquil scene.

說起台北的米粉湯，怎能錯過太原路上林母仔的店的海鮮米粉湯。一大碗公有鮮蝦、干貝、小卷、魚丸，鬆軟米粉吸附了鹹香湯汁，是炒了蝦米、干貝粉與油蔥的湯水滿溢油香嚐起來層次有味，像這樣澎湃海鮮料陣容在小吃攤出現著實少見。

其實以前這裡還有賣麵賣水餃，曾經店內的招牌臭豆腐也有好一陣子停賣了，後來才重返菜單，這裡的臭豆腐是屬於軟皮派系，口感扎實豆香四溢，而清脆台式泡菜酸酸甜甜帶著鮮果香氣。

林母仔的店
Mother Lin's Seafood
Facebook ohma100

台北市大同區太原路 238 號
0919-133-401
15:00-19:00（Sat&Sun 12:00-）

會知道這些，其實是有次現場候位排隊時遇到常來的熟客，還說，老闆娘時常面無表情是因為一人料理太忙，其實人很好的，果不然，離開前正好有機會與老闆娘閒聊幾句，得知林母仔為「你母親」的有趣意思。

原本在一旁的雙連市場內營業，後來才搬遷至現址，前前後後算起來有近四年了，來這的熟客也都非常有默契，知道老闆娘人手不足，吃完都會再自己回收碗筷，這樣互助的心情就像一家人一樣，真的好暖。

When talking about rice noodle soup in Taipei, there's never a time when *Lin Muzi's* is not mentioned. Situated at *Taiyuan Road*, *Mother Lin's* seafood rice noodle soup consists of a big hearty bowl of fresh prawns, scallops, squid, fish balls on a bed of soft and supple rice noodles that perfectly soak up the rich savoury broth. The soup itself is a pork bone broth, stewed with fried and dried shrimps, powdered scallops and shallots. The generous portion size and plentiful variety of seafood served in each bowl makes *Mother Lin* a rare gem in Taipei's sea of street food stalls.

Besides their noodle soup, *Mother Lin's* is famous for their signature stinky tofu which disappeared from its menu for a while but has since returned. *Lin Muzi's* stinky tofu retains a beautifully soft texture even after deep-frying and boasts a strong soybean aroma - an indication of high-quality tofu. Served with their stinky tofu is a side of crispy and tangy pickled cabbages that give a delightfully fruity aroma.

While waiting in the queue, I began talking to another customer who frequented the stall. She mentioned that the owner doesn't smile much because she cooks alone, but she was actually very nice and friendly when it was my turn to order. What's more interesting is that after getting the opportunity to talk to the owner, I learnt that the name of the store actually means "*your mother*" when pronounced in Taiwanese.

Originally found at *Shuanglian Market, Mother Lin's* moved to its current location nearly four years ago and has since developed a strong following of locals who treat the store as a meet up spot. The relationship between the owner and customers are so good that when the store becomes too busy, customers will help tidy up and return bowls and cultery after they're finished with them. It's truly heartwarming to discover this little part of Taipei where the community lives in harmony as one big caring family.

台北大稻埕永樂市場內有間專賣油飯的百年老舖林合發油飯店，每回經過長長隊伍都排到市場門外，時常接近中午就完售。

這裡的油飯是糯米與配料分開拌炒，軟Q粒粒分明且滿溢著麻油香氣，喜氣紅盒先裝油飯再鋪上滿滿肉絲蝦米與香菇等鹹料，豐富了米飯的醇香，光是油飯就已讓人不停回味。再擺進雞腿與紅蛋的澎湃組合，也成了台灣習俗裡的彌月禮盒。

常常中午前買了就帶回家與家人一起分著吃，不需再放進鍋子裡加熱，常溫的口感最好。

林合發油飯店

Lin He Fa Glutinous Rice

台北市大同區迪化街一段 21 號永樂市場 1430 攤位
02-2559-2888
07:30-12:30 closed on Mon

Within Taipei's *Yongle market* at *Dadaocheng*, you'll find the *Lin He Fa Glutinous Rice* that has been serving their specialty *you fan* (Taiwanese glutinous rice) for over 100 years. Like a daily ritual, a long queue builds outside the store, even to the edge of the market, and often they even sell out long before noon.

The *you fan* from here is a plethora of ingredients that have been stir-fried first and then mixed into glutinous rice and steamed together. The rice is mixed until the individual grains of the rice are semi-intact, giving the dish a distinct and desirable chewy texture and the aroma of sesame oil. The *you fan* at *Lin He Fa* is sold in the boxful - *you fan* topped with shredded pork, shrimps, mushrooms and other traditional and savoury ingredients and then wrapped together in their auspicious and recognisable red box. Every bite of the *you fan* is accompanied by a delicious aftertaste that has people back queuing for more. Recently, *Lin He Fa* has also put together a special *you fan* with chicken legs and red-dyed eggs that has become a smash hit with the locals.

When I'm nearby, I usually stop by the hotel just before noon and buy a box to take home and share with my family. Don't worry about re-heating it as it's best eaten at room temperature.

會知道滋生青草店，是有日讀到介紹台北老字號店鋪的書籍介紹，當時想著大稻埕竟有這麼生津解渴又退火的好地方，我怎麼會從來沒試過呢。

滋生青草茶生意有多好，你看一間店騎樓下設置兩站飲料攤就知道。阿姨坐在架高飲料檯上問你要什麼茶，一邊說著：「青草茶降肝火又消暑氣，苦茶清熱解毒抗發炎、茅根茶能降腸氣胃氣」，然後再問你要微糖或無糖、冰的溫的、小杯大杯，與時俱進的多種客製調配，與現今手搖店家相比完全不遑多讓。

老店現已傳承至第四代經營，夏天買茶飲的人多幾乎沒有休息日，冬天則在週日休店。小杯份量正好可以站著喝完再離開，純粹樸實的青草熬煮鮮香又補身，是轉眼已過了百年的光景。

滋生青草店
Zih Sheng Herbal Tea

台北市大同區民樂街 53 號
02-2559-1384
08:00-20:00 closed on Sun

I first learnt about *Zih Sheng*, a traditional herbal tea shop, from a book that introduced some of Taiwan's most time-honoured stores. At the time, I thought, *Dadaocheng* is such a well-known spot for all things beverage related, how come I've never came across this place?

To see how good business can be for a traditional herbal tea store, you need to look no further than downstairs of the store, where you'll find two stalls selling their herbal remedies. The auntie at the stall picked up on my curiosity and asked me what I wanted. "*Our herbal tea reduces irritation and heat, the bitter tea clears heat, reduces inflammation and detoxifies the body, and the mao gen tea is good for reducing intestinal gas and helping strengthen your stomach*" she told me. To keep up with modern beverage stalls, they even offer customisations - how much sugar, without or without ice, small or large and a variety of flavours to choose from.

Zih Sheng is a family business and has been passed down onto its 4th generation of owners. In the summer, its most common patrons are those with a busy work schedule who benefit the most from the tea's health restoring properties. In the winter, the store is less busy and closes on Sundays. One small cup of herbal tea is the perfect size to drink while perching next to the store before leaving. It's amazing to think that one humble cup of herbal tea, drank in no longer than a few minutes, contains more than a hundred years of family-held tradition and expertise.

以紅豆餡為靈魂的滋養豆餡舖，店內首推銅鑼燒、草莓大福與最中，另外鳳梨酥、蜂蜜蛋糕與麻糬也相當受歡迎。老店搬遷至迪化街裡特別規劃一扇現烤「最中」的料理窗口，薄薄酥脆的最中有種米香餅乾感，內餡紅豆份量不少，咬下綿密過癮，據說豆餡已有調降甜度，若依舊覺得甜感較高，正好能佐上現泡的無糖紅茶。

而冬季限定的草莓大福一人一顆剛好，嚐在嘴裡有軟Q麻糬與香氣紅豆餡，使用本地新鮮草莓有著自然果酸甜香。店舖騎樓下總是擺滿長板木凳圓椅，每每大稻埕逛累了，可以走到這坐下，點上一份最中喝點茶，冬日再多一顆草莓大福，舊城旅行最療癒不過如此。

滋養豆餡舖

Lin's Wagashi Confectionery

Facebook wagashi.tw

台北市大同區迪化街一段 247 號
0933-727-553
09:00-19:00

Lin's Wagashi Confectionery is simply a must visit location for their expertly crafted *wagashi* - a Japanese sweet snack, that is intricately crafted into beautiful nuggets of art. *Lin's wagashi* revolves around *anko*, a sweet paste made from softened azuki beans, which form the core of many popular and well known *wagashi*, including *dorayaki* and strawberry *daifuku*. After its relocation to *Dihua street*, a new kitchen area was created for the newly introduced meal set "*monaka*", a type of *wagashi* made of azuki bean paste sandwiched between two thin crisp wafers made from mochi. The chef has reduced the sweetness of the filling if you're not one for sweet desserts. The *wagashi* are best savoured with freshly brewed unsweetened black tea.

In the winter, the store produces their speciality limited edition *strawberry daifuku*, which consists a large strawberry encased in *anko* and wrapped in a skin of silky smooth and soft *mochi*. Every bite is met with a delicious azuki bean aroma and a burst of juicy strawberry that beautifully contrasts with the chew of the *mochi* exterior. Next time when you're in the *Dadaocheng* area, be sure to visit *Lin's* and get yourself a *daifuku* and one of their many excellent teas and spend a moment to sit down and relax.

由福建福州傳至台灣的胡椒餅，是我在台北最愛的烤餅小食。尋尋覓覓台北各家胡椒餅店，總沒有特別上心頭的，恰巧有次在華陰街排隊買甜甜圈時瞄見了斜對角的福元胡椒餅店，於是走了過去一問還有 15 分鐘就出爐，馬上付錢取號碼牌等著，有胡椒餅吃怎能錯過。

現捏的麵皮夾進梅花豬肉與肩頰肉兩種豬肉，再添點黑胡椒與蔥末入味，撒上白芝麻收尾，接著放進窯爐裡可不是時間到就好，炭火大小、天氣濕度等難以捉摸的因素，都會影響餅的熟度與口感，以致出爐時間每次都不同，像是冬天溼冷就得烤久一點，有時上色不完全也要再多等一會兒。

福元胡椒餅

Fu Yuan Peppered Meat Pastry

台北市大同區華陰街 42-19 號
02-2550-0356
12:00-18:30 Closed on Mon&Sun

「現吃小心燙口！」大姐溫馨提醒著。而我迫不及待接過熱騰騰的烤餅，再戰戰兢兢咬開炭香酥脆的外皮，肉塊好扎實好多汁鮮美，帶有胡椒辛香滋味，是難以形容的滿足，於是每次想吃就會特地跑來買上一個，也能提前打電話預約。

從小攤車年代至華陰街外帶賣門店，20 多年的烤餅經驗，真材實料與細心照料的手藝讓福元胡椒餅成了我心中的最愛。

Hujiaobing, the peppery meat-filled pastries baked in a clay oven, are my favourite snacks of all time in Taipei. Originally from the *Fuzhou* province of China, the delicious baked pastry eventually migrated to Taiwan. Having tried many of the *hujiaobing* across the city, none stood out to me as particularly outstanding. One time, while queuing up to buy donuts from a store on *Huayin street*, I happened to notice a store opposite selling *hujiaobing*. Intrigued, I popped over and asked when the next batch would be ready. "*15 minutes*" the owner said, as I eagerly paid and took the number ticket. *How could I not wait 15 minutes for such a delicious snack?*

batch of *hujiaobing*. In the winter, the pastries require longer baking times as the dough begins colder and is more wet. It's not uncommon to be told that you'll have to spend longer waiting in front of the store, but worth it every time.

"*Eat it while it's hot, but be careful you don't burn yourself!*" the lady told me as the passed me the piping hot *hujiaobing*. I couldn't resist waiting any longer as I took a bite through the crispy smoky pastry. The juice inside flowed out of the pastry revealing a mouthful of delicious peppery pork filling. There are honestly no words to describe the

Hujiaobing are pastries made from freshly kneaded dough, stuffed with a mix of pork shoulder and cheek meat, chopped spring onions and most importantly, a generous sprinkle of black pepper that delivers a potent and characteristic kick. After each pastry is made, it's embossed with a coat of white sesame, and impressively slapped onto the inside of a large clay oven overhanging the charcoal fire that gives it its delicious smoky aroma. How long the dough has been proofed for, the consistency and composition of the filling and the temperature of the oven itself are all factors that play a part in determining the quality of each

satisfaction that comes from trying a freshly baked *hujiaobing*. Every time I'm in the area and think of their *hujiaobing*, I find myself slowly building up speed in their direction. If you're on your way to get one, you'll be glad to know that you can also call to find out when the next batch is ready and reserve one in advance.

Starting out from a stall to now a permanent store located on *Huayin street*, Fuyuan has had more than 20 years of experience in making *hujiaobing* from high quality ingredients, placing them at the top of my list for must visit locations.

藏身於民宅狹巷裡的門前隱味，3 坪大的空間只有 5 張座位，一日最多只賣 30 碗麵，這裡受歡迎的程度是目前預約已排至 2023 年 11 月了，一碗牛肉麵 3 年後才吃得到的約定，是既瘋狂卻又真實。

以新鮮番茄加上洋蔥等食材純天然燉煮的湯頭，算算從第一天同鍋燉煮至今已風味堆疊累積 1300 多個日子了，這樣的做法讓味道每天都有點微妙變化，濃郁湯汁也像是伴隨著時間一起記憶，越久越是層次香醇。這裡還有自己最掛念的豆干，切得特別薄片是需要醃製 3 天才能端上桌的，那爽口迷人的入味香氣，聽說是來自大叔媽媽的手藝。除了用心的家常味外，這裡的靈魂還有那溫暖的大叔，他讓吃一碗牛肉麵的時間，不再是簡單溫飽的 10 分鐘，而是慢慢品嚐，有著更多回憶相伴。

門前隱味

Wumamii

www.wumamii.com.tw
Instagram wumamiiig

02-2700-8937
新北市板橋區四川路一段 87 巷 2 弄 12-2 號 1 樓
reservation only

Hidden in a narrow alley of a private residence with only five seats in a ten square meter space and serving only 30 bowls of noodles each day, *Wumamii* is truly a hidden gem of the Taipei food scene. Reservation only, and fully booked until November 2023, what seems like just a simple bowl of beef noodle soup that can only be eaten after waiting for three years seems unbelievable, but true!

The noodles that are served by *Wumamii* is not just a hype - each bowl contains the essence and flavour of a remarkable tomato and onion broth that has been stewing and accumulating in intensity for more than 1300 days since the pot was first started. This method of cooking results in the taste changing on a daily basis as the flavours mellow and intensify over time.

Also served on the menu is the Taiwanese dried beancurd that I miss the most. Each piece of beancurd is marinaded for three days in their special sauce and sliced thin before serving. Each bowl of soup represents perfectly what you'd expect from a recipe that was passed down from the owner's mother.

In addition to the home-cooked feeling that is imbued into every bowl, the friendly owner also makes you feel at home. The feeling within each bowl of noodle transcends the 10 minutes that you spend eating it - it's not just about eating when hungry, but is truly a moment worth savouring.

若問淡水名產有哪些？眾所皆知是古早味阿給、鐵蛋或魚丸；我們則偏心鄰近眞理大學山波甜點店的羊焦糖戚風，是柔潤蛋糕夾上新鮮熬煮 3 小時的羊乳焦糖醬，再淋上幾匙的鮮奶油清爽，那香甜別緻的滋味是別處怎樣都遍尋不著的。

最近一次，試了將大黃入甜的大黃派，與蘋果肉餡酸甜醇厚層層交織也很是特別。不僅甜點，山波出杯的飲品也很有看頭，從沒遇過拿實體蜂窩當搭配的泰式拿鐵，一口蜂窩、再一口咖啡，原來太美早已不足以形容山波，而是色、香、味、形、意面面俱全的出色。兩人作業的小店，著實佩服小鈞和翁姐能不時推出創意又唯美的新品；是堅持完美的心意，來款待遠道而來的有緣人。

原來，淡水不只離海好近，也能嚐到餘味悠久的香甜滋味。

山波

Simple Dessert

Instagram simple_tw

新北市淡水區新民街 180 巷 7 弄 43 號
02-2625-3118
13:00-19:00（不定休）

What are the most famous products from *Tamsui*? Everyone talks about the Taiwanese-style "*A-gei*" (a Taiwanese stuffed tofu snack), the famous *Tamsui* "*iron egg*" (stewed eggs) or the fish balls, but we prefer the goat-milk caramel chiffon that you can buy from *Simple Dessert* near the *Tamsui Aletheia University*. The cake sold here is a deliciously light and fluffy chiffon infused with the flavour of goat's milk and caramel, and topped with a generous dollop of cream. Try finding this combination somewhere else!

The last time I visited *Simple Dessert,* I tried the rhubarb pie, fused with layers of sweet and tart apple filling. The beverages on the menu are also highly recommended. Have you ever encountered a Thai-style latté with actual honeycombs? As it turns out, a mouthful of honeycomb and another of coffee pairs surprisingly well. The colour, fragrance, taste, shape and atmosphere of *Simple Dessert* are truly outstanding.

Co-founders Hsiaojun and Miss Weng are idealists that love a creative twist to a traditional dessert. The duo are perfectionists that don't want to disappoint any of their customers who travel far for their creations. After stumbling upon *Simple Dessert*, we realised that *Tamsui* is worth visiting for much more than just a view of the ocean.

記憶裡，好多次一到瑞芳就開始下起細雨，灰濛濛細雨的山城雖有另一種淒幽之美，但撐著傘總少了點閒逛的興致，想著此時若能坐下嚐碗熱騰騰的雞湯該有多好啊！而金瓜石裡的迷迷路食堂正好讓如我們一般貪嘴愛幻想的旅人總算得以如願以償了。

午後滿室人聲熱鬧著，偶爾聽見廚房傳來器皿堆疊的聲響，坐在窗旁像是能聞見山林呼吸的氣息，也特別涼快。窗外依山而立是從前各戶人家的樓房，太多已上了年紀，早荒廢了，感覺只有為數不多像迷迷路食堂一樣重新將百年老房換上新色，在山中生活著。

迷迷路食堂
Take A Walk Diner

新北市瑞芳區祈堂街 150 號
Fri-Sun 11:30-15:30（Last order 14:30）

這裡營業日限量供應 30 份雞肉料理，以五菜一湯套餐呈現。蓮藕浸漬了柚香，地瓜切成方形疊起再灑上芝麻與調味粉，份量不多的小菜每道竟是如此費心，麵條拌開咬著扎實油香，細熬慢燉的雞湯料理，嚐到肉的軟嫩，與清雅細緻的湯頭韻味，飯後還有甜點和飲品，很是豐盛飽足的一餐。

8 年前，店主馬丁先生因為改造老屋，一路自學開啓了與瑞芳小鎮的奇妙緣份，至今已改造六棟在地老房，每一個過程著實都替山中帶來更多溫暖光亮，而迷迷路食堂的雞湯，從此也成了我們旅行瑞芳最暖心的歇腳特產。

My memory of *Ruifang* is one that always seems to involve rain. Don't get me wrong, *Ruifang*, regarded as a secluded beauty, is still worth exploring even amidst all the grey and rain, but hanging out with an umbrella isn't the most interesting. If I could choose one place to hide away from the rain, I would definitely say *Take a Walk Diner* in *Jinguashih* - oh how good a bowl of hot chicken soup can be! This place really is every foodie's dream come true!

By the afternoon, the diner was packed with people and the kitchen alive with the clinging

sweet potatoes, arranged into a tidy cubic stack and garnished with a generous sprinkling of nutty sesame and seasoning, and wax apples infused with the flavour of grapefruit. The star of the show is a hearty bowl of rich chicken soup bursting with flavour. The tenderness of the chicken and the sweetness of the soup perfectly ties together the elegance of the set. Every dish in this meal is perfectly executed.

The story of *Take a Walk Diner* started eight years ago when the owner Martin, decided to take over the old building that now houses the diner, and

and clanging of busy chefs. Sitting by the window, you can see and almost smell the mountains, showering in the seasonal downpour. Lower down, the trees are underlined by rows of old buildings, like neat vegetation, but housing family trees with roots engrained into the past. Many of these buildings are old and barren, and few have had the chance to be refurbished into the 21st century.

On busy days, the diner offers only 30 of their highly sought-after set meals, which include five dishes and one soup. The side dishes include

develop it into the talk of the town. Since then, he has renovated a total of six buildings across the town, with each renewal breathing new life into *Ruifang*. The chicken soup from the *Take a Walk Diner* has definitely become one of the main reasons that we enjoy travelling to *Ruifang*.

當車子緩緩駛上蜿蜒瑞金公路，搖搖晃晃好不容易抵達九份老街，這時就該用心念許久的食物好好慰勞自己一番，喜歡排隊買幾個阿蘭草仔粿，然後吃碗郵局對面層層手作油蔥粿，接著坐下歇腳看山看海佐上 Q 滑芋圓，已像是約定俗成的安排了。

從小在台北長大，拜訪九份的次數早已不計其數。然而發覺九份在自己人生每個階段皆留下不同的印象，懵懂孩提可能視野有限只記得老街裡賣著古玩和傳統小吃；等到上了大學，才曾有過留宿一夜，腦海深刻是俯瞰繁華燈影消散與晨曦濛濛時光；現在，或許因為心境慢了，反倒流連於山城

九份老街
Jiufen Old Street

新北市瑞芳區基山街
08:00-22:00

裡的生活民情與幽幽氣息。

九份崎嶇山路卻樓房層層比鄰而建，其實可想而知這裡過去因礦產有多繁華，而後產業瞬時變遷，許多屋舍商家成了如今廢墟，直至 20 年前成立九份觀光商圈，也在電影《悲情城市》的助攻下，才再次替山鎮帶來一點熱鬧。

現在的九份，有奇麗的建築，古老的滋味，是歲月遺留下的小城。餘味悠久的古道小徑，也成為到訪旅人，尋探過去百年繁華的時光入口。

Driving to *Jiufen* is always a perilous journey - not because of the winding roads of the *Ruijin highway*, but because of all the thoughts of the food that accumulate in your mind while driving there! It's only when your car finally reaches the *Jiufen Old Street*, that you'll be convinced that those thoughts will be realised soon.

The first thing I do when I arrive, is queue up to grab a few '*cao ah kueh*' (iconic traditional Taiwanese-Hakka stuffed glutinous rice dumpling) from *Alan's* and then head across from the post office for some of the handmade shallot'*kueh*'(glutinous rice dumpling). To satisfy my sweet tooth, I'll visit one of *Jiufen's* many stores that sell '*yu yuan*' - sweet and chewy glutinous taro balls, while taking in the view of the mountains and the sea. It's like a customary tradition each time I visit now.

Growing up in Taipei, I've visited *Jiufen* more times than I can count. Each time I visit however, *Jiufen* leaves a different impression on me as I grow older.

The serpentine roads of *Jiufen* meander unrestrainedly across the steep mountainside, inlaid with a patchwork of mismatched buildings. Driving through here, you really get a sense of history - how the area developed as a prosperous mining town, rich with mineral deposits. Abruptly, the industry stopped, but the fire of *Jiufen* was rekindled by the popularity of a movie called "*A City of Sadness*", which revitalised the old sleepy mining town into a touristic hotspot.

Jiufen is home to a wonderful array of architecture, telling the story of a bygone era. The town is small, but the roads and buildings are rich and deep with history and serves as the first calling point for many tourists in their exploration of Taiwan's path to prosperity over the last century.

OUT OF TOWN 城外

SPOT

新北市瑞芳區基山街 90 號
02-2496-7795
09:00－20:30

新北市瑞芳區基山街 111 號
02-2497-6393
10:00-17:00（Sat&Sun-18:00）

新北市瑞芳區豎崎路 5 號
02-2497-6505
09:00-20:00（Sat-22:00）

福隆，是小時候對於大海的記憶，曾經因此以為海邊就是撒上金黃色海砂，直至長大後才明白，金黃細沙是如此獨特。

福隆，是台北人夏季的天然戲水池，每到貢寮國際海洋音樂祭與沙雕藝術節就擠滿了人，這裡是貢寮的下一站，從台北搭火車一個多小時抵達。

留在腦海裡的福隆很熱鬧，還有車站外兩側擺滿的繽紛戲水用具；來這餓了一定要吃當地名產福隆便當，有控肉瘦肉雙拼，再放上香腸、滷蛋與高麗菜組合，這樣古早賣樣滋味是搭車返家前的最後療癒；而啤酒更是想盡興而歸不可少的旅伴，屢試不爽。

福隆海水浴場

Fulong Beach

新北市貢寮區福隆街 41 號
02-2563-8780
08:00-18:00（L.A. 17:30），08:00-18:30（L.A. 18:00）（Sat&Sun）

Fulong, is my memory of a child meeting the big sea for the first time. A child that once thought that all beaches were made from a sprinkling of gold sand. It wasn't until I grew up and visited other beaches, that I came to realise that the golden sands of *Fulong* were so unique.

Fulong is a natural paddling pool for busy Taipei people during the summer months. Each time the *Ho-hai-yan Rock Festival* and *Sand Sculpture Art Festival* starts nearby, the beaches of *Fulong* are alive with the energy of beach-goers as it takes only an hour to get to by train from Taipei.

Imagining *Fulong* now, brings to mind the summer warmth, and the rows of stalls either side of the train station, packed with colourful beach toys. On your next trip here, be sure to try the local famous *Fulong bento* before travel back to Taipei, which consists of braised lean pork and pork belly, traditional sausages, soy-marinaded eggs and crisp Taiwanese cabbage. Grab a beer on the way back to complete the perfect getaway.

站在馬路旁等著店家開門時，無聊端詳了建築體外觀，這才發現「啊！原來這是一棟水泥鐵皮老房，在設計師的巧思設計下，以沉穩色調板材外飾，兩層樓的綠河遠看還頗有日本木造家屋町家的味道。」

十一點一到咖啡師下樓開門，親切地引領所有人上樓「有空位都能坐」，挑高二樓讓空間感受特別寬敞，灰色尖屋頂加上米色木條除了懸掛吊燈外，也與整體木質調相呼應，從木材吧檯家具，到木紋地板運用，都讓人沉浸在自然舒適的溫暖氣息裡。

綠河
Green River Roastery
Instagram greenriverroastery

新北市新店區環河路 100 號
11:00-19:00 closed on Tue

L 型吧檯有著兩扇小窗，是陽光穿過霧濛視線與綠意問好；陽台迎向蓊鬱可以放空頭腦；而一點異素材混搭讓空間不只平靜也能感到有趣跳躍，原本閒置於新店馬路旁的舊屋，在悉心改造下有了嶄新的生命體，真的太好。

而這裡咖啡甜點也挺好；甚至離開這裡肚子若餓徒步 8 分鐘還有一家鵝肉專賣店，那鵝肉鵝腸好鮮好嫩，再沾點蒜油更好，總之，下次還想再這樣鹹的甜的一次都嚐到。

While waiting for the store to open, a bored me took a look around the exterior of the building, only to discover that it was converted from one of the city's old cement and iron houses, now disguised in a palette of calm, minimal tones and clad in complementary wooden panels. From a distance, the two storey building still has the distinctive aura of a Japanese *machiya*.

At 11:00, a barista appeared and opened the front door for business. Upstairs is where you'll find the seating area - a high-ceiling interior which makes the space feel particularly spacious. Beige wooden slats run along the grey gable roof, with chandeliers hanging high above and illuminating the room. Like its facade, the interior is decorated in wooden furniture and wooden floors that exude a natural and comforting atmosphere.

The L-shaped bar has two small windows where the outside greenery occasionally peeks through to spy on the customers. The sun kissed balcony offers the perfect environment for a relaxing afternoon. It's remarkable to think that a sleepy old house could be transformed into such a comfortable and interesting point of interest after a little but careful renovation.

Green River's coffees and desserts are excellent. If you're hungry after visiting the roastery, there's a store a short walk away that specialises in goose dishes, perfect with a good slather of chili oil. Why not pop by next time you're nearby to get your fix of both sweet and savoury in one go?

只有區間車行經的三貂嶺站，走過溪邊穿越地下道，在近橋倚山的層層舊房裡有一處開放給過路旅人與小貓休憩的 Cafe Hytte，小橘子、虎皮捲、Kiki 三隻小貓天天都會來作客，所以店家早已安排好空位。

咖啡館沒有太過張揚的改造，水泥廢墟結構先以舊石料堆上一邊圍牆，再蓋上原木屋頂，鋪上木料地板，一張長木桌得以準備幾款咖啡，偶爾幾款甜食，就過起想要的生活。

Cafe Hytte

Instagram cafehytte

新北市瑞芳區魚寮路 113 號
11:00-17:00（no restroom provided）

在這喝了熱拿鐵與熱卡布有深焙豆的醇厚；來自友人媽媽手藝的奶油捲則溢滿了幸福香甜。屋外的空間是枝葉蔓生，自由的氣息瀰漫滿室，想著哪天到訪時若是幸運晴天，最愜意，必是坐在屋外與山與水與土好近的滋味。

這裡是平溪小鎮裡的咖啡島嶼，來了你就會明白，離世的廢墟咖啡館，反而是與生活好近的一種姿態，一種味道。

—

※ 前往 Cafe Hytte 前，記得先詳細閱讀主人明訂的規則，若只是想踩點拍照、不喝咖啡、不珍惜食物，一定會被婉拒在門外。

Cafe Hytte is located within a secluded part of town, situated inside of an old building leaning on the side of a mountain. The closest station is *Sandiaoling* which is only accessible via a local train operated by Taiwan Railway. The cafe serves as a resting point for weary travellers, hikers and three small kittens - "*little orange*", "*tiger skin*" and Kiki, who visit every day to greet the customers. Be careful you don't take their seats!

Renovated from a rustic cement building surrounded by fences made from remodelled stone, the cafe itself is sandwiched between a wooden roof and wooden floor. On the menu are a selection of coffees, beers, sparkling water and some homemade fine desserts. The cafe's coffees are of the strong, dark-roast variety - the perfect concoction to revitalise its tired guests. Offset the bold and nutty flavours with a swiss roll, freshly baked by the owner's mother.

A long wooden table stretches across the courtyard, providing space for its guests to get some air. In the nice weather, a quiet seat outside in the tranquil courtyard, surrounded by the natural greenery is often all you need for a good rest before you continue your travels.

One of nature's gems, hidden away in Taipei, *Cafe Hytte* represents the unblemished charm of a natural environment within a busy urban capital.

-

※Before visiting *Cafe Hytte*, make sure to familiarise yourself with the rules set out by the owner - guests who only visit for instagrammable shots and waste food are not welcome!

台北多謝
陪你旅行當道地的台霸郎

作者	男子的日常生活
主編	王衣卉
行銷企劃	王綾翊
英文翻譯	曾維宏、Andy Lau
英文審訂	曾維宏、Andy Lau
封面設計	謝捲子
內頁設計	Rika Su

第五編輯部總監	梁芳春
董事長	趙政岷
出版者	時報文化出版企業股份有限公司
	108019 台北市和平西路三段二四〇號

發行專線	(02)2306-6842
讀者服務專線	(02)2304-7013、0800-231-705
郵撥	19344724 時報文化出版公司
信箱	10899 臺北華江橋郵局第 99 信箱
時報悅讀網	www.readingtimes.com.tw
電子郵件信箱	yoho@readingtimes.com.tw
法律顧問	理律法律事務所　陳長文律師、李念祖律師
印刷	和楹印刷有限公司
初版一刷	2021 年 5 月 14 日
定價	新臺幣 650 元

台北多謝 / 男子的日常生活著 . -- 初
版 . -- 臺北市 : 時報文化出版企業股份
有限公司 , 2021.05
224 面 ; 19x26 公分
中英對照
ISBN 978-957-13-8959-2(平裝)

1. 遊記 2. 臺北市 3. 新北市

733.9/101.69　　　　　110006703

時報文化出版公司成立於一九七五年，並於一九九九年股票上櫃公開發行，於二〇〇八年脫離中時集團非屬旺中，以「尊重智
慧與創意的文化事業」為信念。